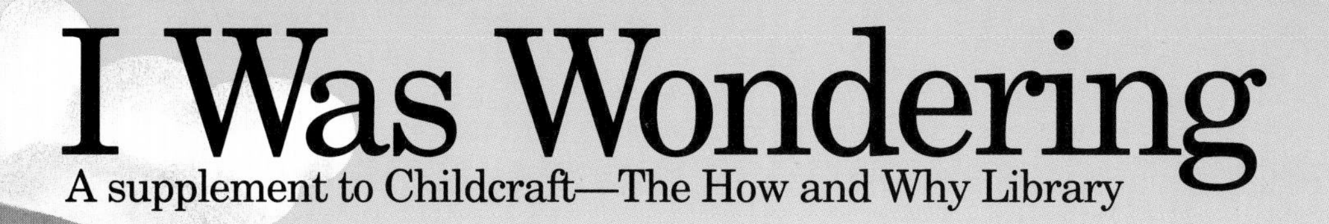

I Was Wondering

A supplement to Childcraft—The How and Why Library

World Book, Inc.
a Scott Fetzer company

Chicago London Sydney Toronto

World Book, Inc.
525 West Monroe St.
Chicago, Illinois 60661

Printed in the United States of America
ISBN 0-7166-0691-7
Library of Congress Catalog Card No. 65-25105

Acknowledgments

The publishers of *Childcraft—The How and Why Library* gratefully acknowledge the courtesy of the following publishers, agencies, authors, and organizations for permission to use copyrighted poems, stories, and illustrations in this volume. Full illustration acknowledgments appear on page 250.

HarperCollins, Inc.: "Wild Strawberries" from *A Light in the Attic.* Copyright © 1981 by Snake Eye Music, Inc. Reprinted by permission of HarperCollins, Inc., and Jonathan Cape.

Henry Holt and Company, Inc.: "Why There Are Four Seasons in the Year," from *The Earth Is on a Fish's Back* by Natalia Belting. Copyright © 1965 by Natalia Belting. Reprinted by permission of Henry Holt and Company, Inc.

"Hide and Seek Shadow," by Margaret Hillert, from *Farther Than Far.* Copyright © 1969. Used by permission by the author, who controls all rights.

Sandra Liastos: "Sea Wave." Used by permission of the author. First appeared in *Ranger Rick* magazine in April 1980, published by the National Wildlife Federation. Secondly appeared in *The Sea Is Calling Me,* by Lee Bennett Hopkins (ed.) in 1986; published by Harcourt Brace Jovanovich, Inc.

Lothrop, Lee & Shepard Books, a division of William Morrow and Co., Inc.: "Is It Alive?" adapted from *Hobie Hanson, You're Weird,* by Jamie Gilson. Copyright © 1987 by Jamie Gilson. Reprinted by permission of William Morrow & Company, Inc.

Macmillan, Inc.: "Can I Grow Freckles?" adapted from *Freckle Juice* by Judy Blume. Copyright © 1971 by Judy Blume. Reprinted by permission of Macmillan, Inc. and Octopus Publishing Group Library.

Lilian Moore: "To the Skeleton of a Dinosaur in a Museum," Copyright © 1979 by Lilian Moore. Reprinted by permission of Marian Reiner for the author.

William Morrow & Company, Inc.: "Rainbows" from *Vacation Time.* Copyright © 1980 by Nikki Giovanni. Reprinted by permission of William Morrow & Company, Inc.

Anita E. Posey: "When All the World's Asleep." Reprinted by permission of Anita E. Posey.

Norma Anchin Untermeyer: "Questions at Night," from *Rainbow in the Sky.* Copyright © 1935 by Harcourt Brace Jovanovich, Inc. Renewed 1963 by Louis Untermeyer. Reprinted by permission of Professional Publishing Services for the author's estate.

Contents

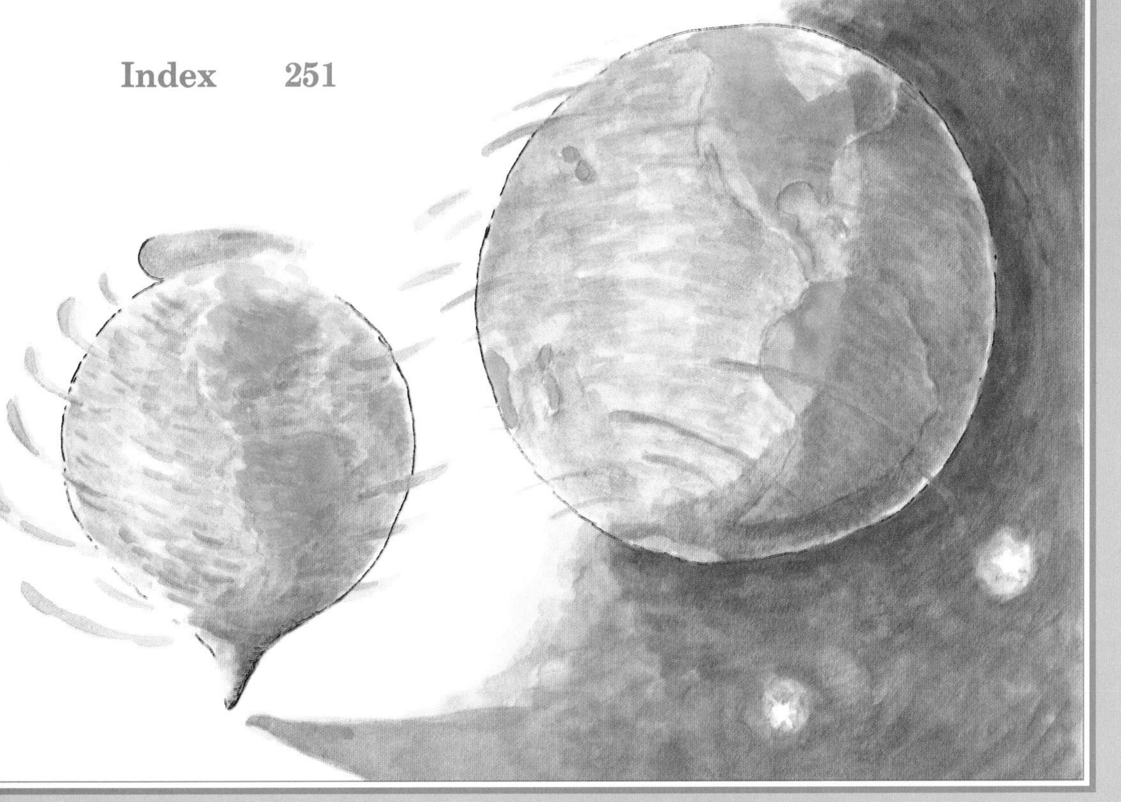

Editorial Advisory Board

for Childcraft–The How and Why Library

The publisher wishes to thank Dr. Paul Heltne, President of the Chicago Academy of Sciences, Chicago, Illinois, for his gracious assistance in reviewing the manuscript of *I Was Wondering;* and Ms. Lisa Hofman and students at Pritchett Elementary School in Buffalo Grove, Illinois, for their enthusiastic assistance in testing the Simple Science activities.

Staff

Preface

Have you ever wondered where snowflakes come from, or how spiders spin webs, or why earthquakes happen? Have you ever wondered what makes your hair grow or why you're ticklish? Wonders are everywhere, and finding out about them is fun!

This book takes a look at wondering. Mainly, it answers many of the questions that children like you ask. The stories and poems show the funny side of wondering. The folk tales show what imagination people brought to their wondering questions long ago. The "simple science" activities help you answer some wondering questions through experiments.

Look around you. Ask some questions. Read and enjoy the book. Most of all—keep on wondering!

The Wonder of Me!

Ah-Choo! Why Do We Sneeze?

Are you a loud sneezer or a quiet, dainty sneezer? Do you sneeze only once, sometimes twice, or many times in a row? Different people sneeze in different ways. Doctors don't really know why. Some say it's probably just habit. But one thing is certain—everyone sneezes. Have you ever wondered why?

A sneeze is a reflex. It is something your body does that you can't control. It just happens. But it happens for a reason. A sneeze protects you.

Getting ready for a sneeze!

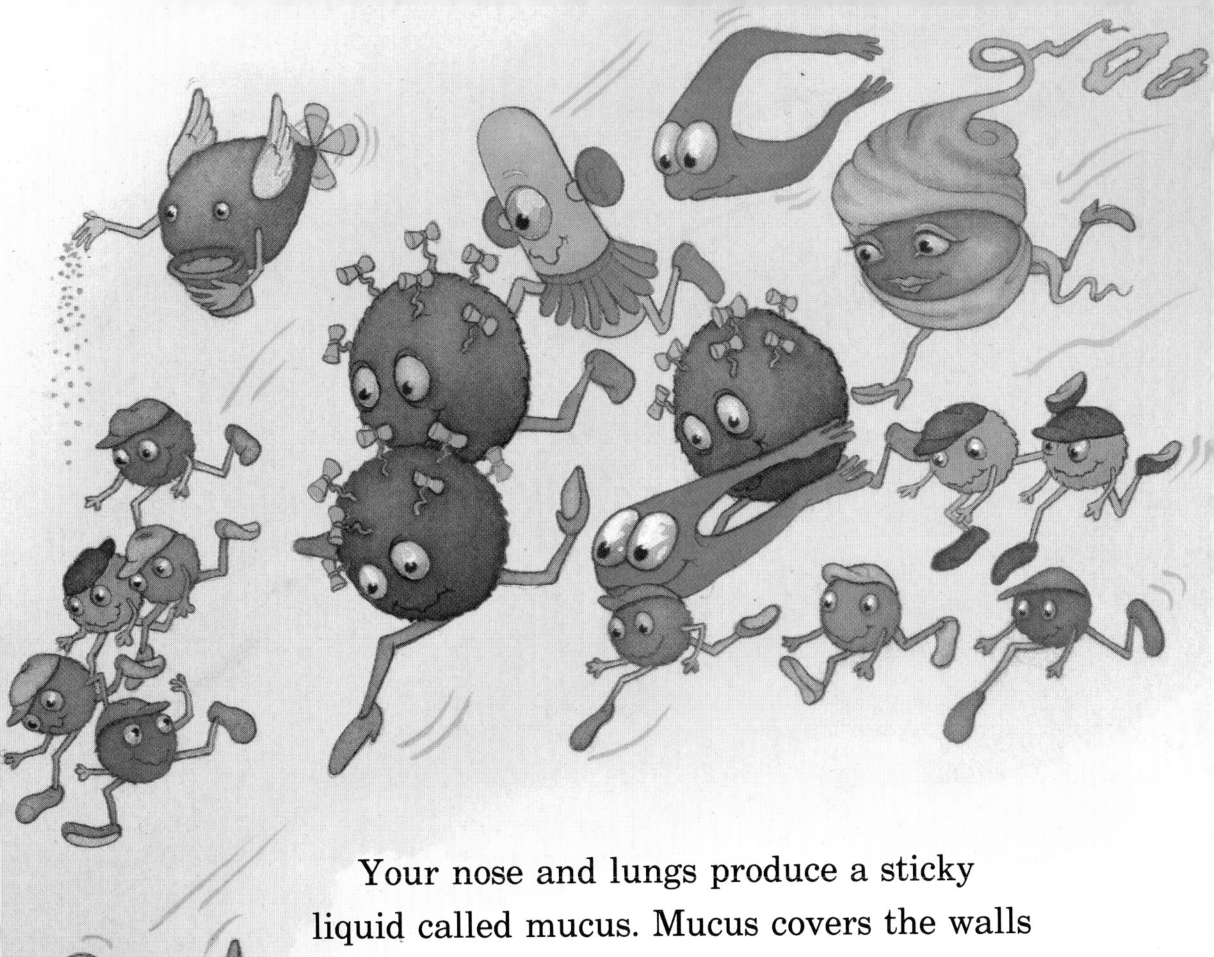

Your nose and lungs produce a sticky liquid called mucus. Mucus covers the walls of your nasal cavity—that is, the tunnel behind your nose. Mucus serves an important purpose. Because it is sticky, it helps trap dust and dirt that you breathe in before it can get to your lungs.

When this dust and dirt collects and bothers the inside of your nose, you sneeze. Germs and bacteria, a certain smell, smoke from chimneys, or fumes from cars can also bother your nose. People with hay fever are often bothered by pollen or other tiny bits of matter, called particles, from trees, grass, and flowers. These particles, though you can't see them, float through the air and

you breathe them in. When you have a cold, the lining of your nose and lungs swells and makes more mucus than usual. This swelling can be irritating to your nose, too.

Whatever the cause, the tiny nerves in your nose sense that something is wrong and they send a message to the brain. The brain tells your body to take a deep breath and fill your lungs with air. That's the *aaaah* part of the sneeze. Then your chest muscles squeeze your chest very hard, sending a blast of air up from your lungs and out of your nose and mouth. That's the *choo* part. The dust, dirt, or other irritating particles are blown out of your nose with the air.

A sneeze is your body's way of getting rid of whatever is bothering your nose.

The explosion of air that forms a sneeze is very powerful. The air may burst out of your nose and mouth at a speed of about 100 miles (160 kilometers) an hour. Long ago, people thought sneezing was a sign that the sneezer was in danger, perhaps of dying. That's how the saying "God bless you" began.

Now we know that sneezes are not dangerous, but spreading germs from a sneeze is not exactly healthful, either. So remember to cover your nose and mouth the next time your nose "explodes." Your family and friends, and anyone else in your path, will be grateful!

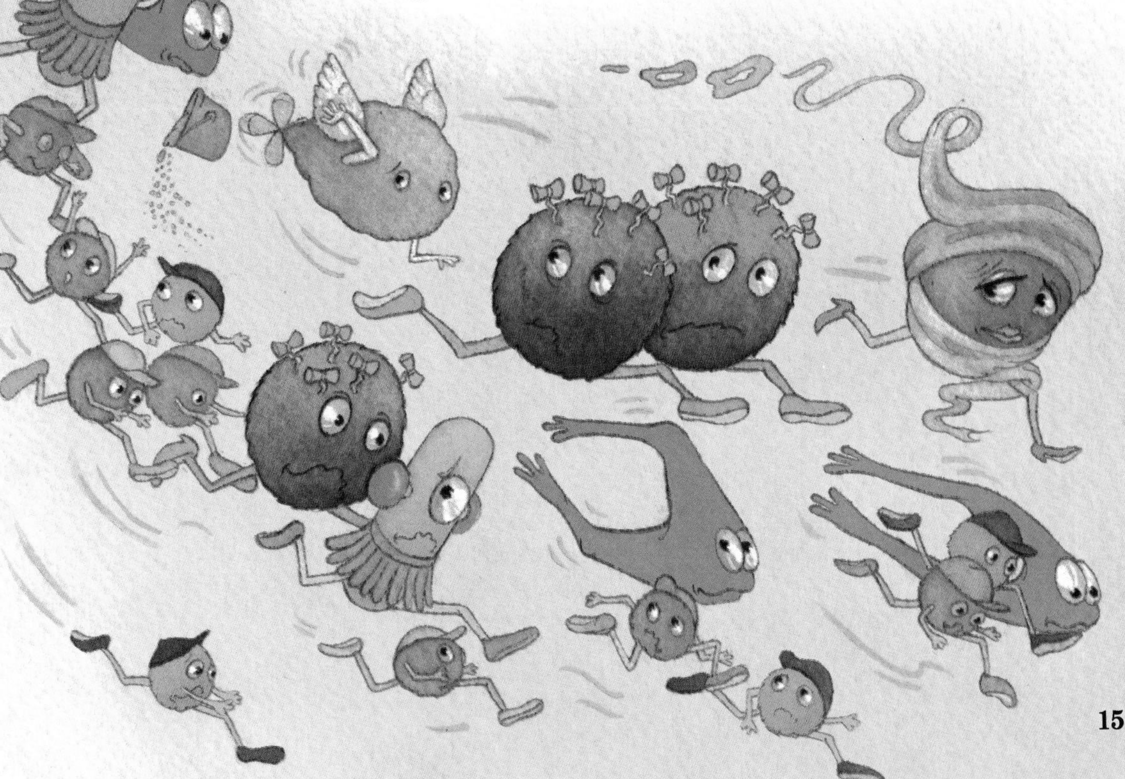

How Come I'm Ticklish?

Where are you most ticklish? Under your arms? Around your middle? Maybe the bottom of your feet? You're not ticklish at all, you say? Some people claim they aren't ticklish. Maybe they are just better at concentrating and not laughing than the rest of us.

Did you ever wonder why you can't help giggling when someone gently moves their fingers on your body? Doctors and scientists don't completely understand tickling. But they do have some ideas about it.

"She'd better stop that tickling soon!"

There are very fine nerve endings that lie just beneath the surface of the skin. These nerve endings are sensitive to the lightest of touches, such as a feather or a tiny bug crawling up your arm. These are the nerves that make you feel an itch or a tickle.

You will usually start laughing when someone tickles you. Some experts think the reason you laugh when you're tickled is

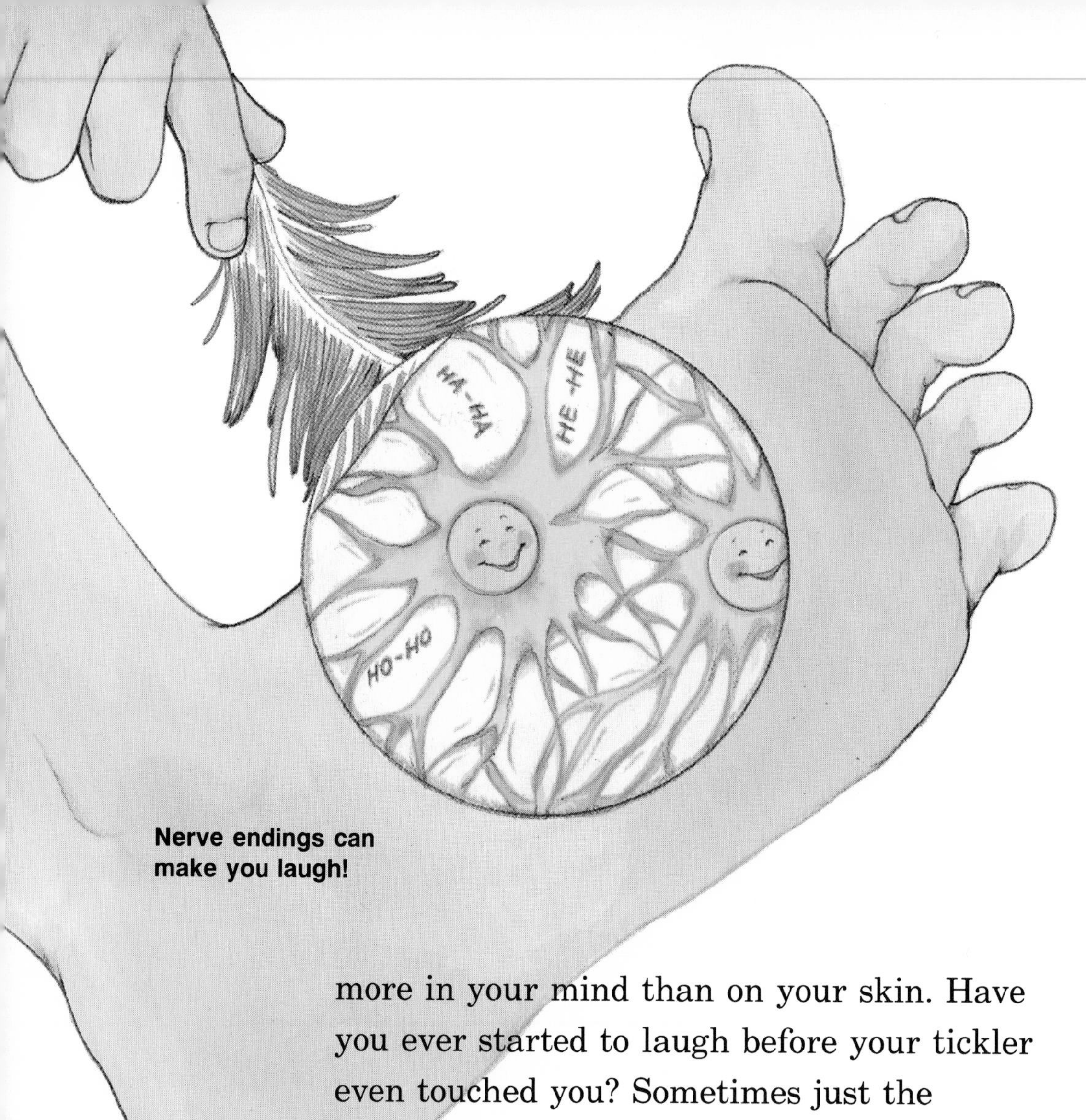

Nerve endings can make you laugh!

more in your mind than on your skin. Have you ever started to laugh before your tickler even touched you? Sometimes just the waiting and knowing that those tickling fingers are approaching make you giggle.

Do you ever get tickled too much? It's not so much fun then. If your brother or sister, for instance, won't stop when you ask, the tickling can almost become painful. Some doctors believe that tickling is only pleasant as long as you trust your tickler. So beware all you ticklers: keep it fun and don't overdo!

Just Wondering

Why Can't I Tickle Myself?

A good question! No one really knows the answer, either. If you try to tickle yourself, you know where your tickle will land and that takes the surprise out. That's one idea. But experimenters found that even when people knew when and where a tickle would come, most of them still laughed when someone *else* tickled them.

If you try to tickle yourself you have all the control, and it's not so much of an "attack" by someone else. The excitement of trying to get away or stopping the tickling isn't there. And without the excitement, we just don't laugh.

What do you think?

Freckles and Why We Have Them

Every summer, Curtis wins the freckle-counting contest at his neighborhood fair. He loves the stuffed animal and the free pizza coupons that are his prize. But he *does not* love the freckles—all 243 of them.

"They make me look like a pet puppy," he complained. "Why can't I get rid of them?" When Curtis was much younger, he tried to scrub them away. It didn't work.

"Freckles are part of your skin color," his dad explained. "You have them because I have them. That means they're hereditary (huh REHD uh ter ee)."

"You don't have them now," replied Curtis.

"No, not as many, but I used to when I was your age," Dad explained. "When people get to be about 20 years old, they usually stop getting freckles. You have a checkup with Doctor Phillips next week. Maybe he can tell you more about freckles."

Curtis learned some interesting things about freckles from the doctor.

First of all, everyone's skin makes a substance called melanin (MEHL uh nihn). Melanin is the brown pigment or coloring

Nancy
Curtis
Stewart
Sally
Uncle Clarence
Aunt Jane
Mom
Dad
Grandpa
Grandma
Great Gramma & Grampa
Great Gramp & Grandma
Our Family Tree

that determines the color of your skin. Darker-skinned people have more melanin than lighter-skinned people. The amount of melanin each person has is set by heredity.

Do you use sunscreen or sun block lotions on your skin? They protect you from the sun's most harmful rays.

That means it was passed to you from your parents before you were born.

In some people, melanin is not spread out evenly over the skin but rather builds up in spots. These spots are freckles. Freckles are just patches of skin that have more melanin than the rest of your skin.

Freckles most often show up on your face, hands, and arms. This is probably because these parts of your body are most often touched by sunlight. The sun causes your skin to make more melanin. That's how you get suntanned. But, if you have freckles, the sun will also increase the melanin spots that become freckles. Usually, people with freckles are very light skinned and don't tan easily. Their freckles increase while the rest of their skin stays light.

"That's why I have more freckles in the summertime," Curtis said.

"That's right," Doctor Phillips replied. "You could stay out of the sun to prevent some freckles."

"Mom always makes me use sun block to protect my skin from the sun," Curtis announced. "But there's no way I want to stay out of the sun during summer. I'd miss out on too much fun. Besides, I'm getting to like free pizza."

Can I Grow Freckles?

adapted from Freckle Juice, *by Judy Blume*

Andrew Marcus wanted freckles, just like Nicky Lane, who sat in front of him in school. Day after day, Andrew would try to count the freckles on the back of Nicky's neck. He could stop doing this and concentrate better in school—and maybe his mother wouldn't make him wash his neck so often—if he just had his own freckles!

"Psst . . . I know how to get freckles," Sharon whispered to Andrew as the class filed out of the room one day. Sharon had heard Andrew ask Nicky about where his freckles came from. "Do you want to know how to get them?"

"Maybe," Andrew told her.

"It'll cost you fifty cents. I have a secret recipe for freckle juice," Sharon whispered.

"A secret recipe?"

"Uh huh."

"But you don't even have freckles!" Andrew continued.

"Look close," Sharon said. "I've got six on my nose."

"Big deal! A lot of good six'll do."

"You can get as many as you want. It all depends on how much freckle juice you drink."

Andrew didn't believe Sharon for a minute. But that night he kept thinking about the freckle juice. Maybe the reason no one in his family had freckles was because no one knew the secret recipe. If they never even heard of freckle juice, then how could they have any freckles? It figured! He didn't like the idea of paying Sharon for anything. But he decided that if the recipe didn't work, he'd ask for his money back. It was easy.

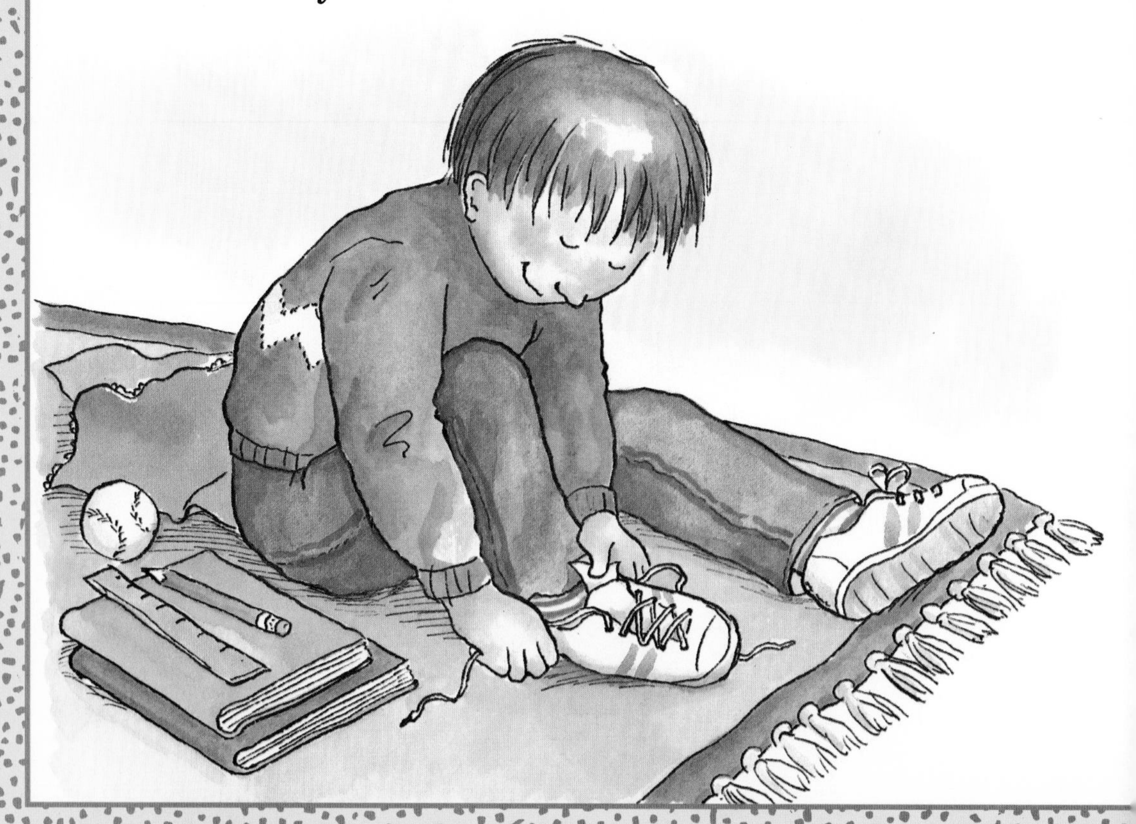

The next day after school, Andrew ran all the way home. The secret recipe for freckle juice was folded carefully in the bottom of his shoe. He made up his mind not to read it until he got home. Dashing to the front door, he let himself in and took off his shoe as soon as he was inside. He pulled out the secret recipe and sat down on the floor to read it. It said:

Sharon's Secret Recipe for Freckle Juice

One glass makes an average amount of freckles. To get like Nicky Lane drink two glasses, mix up all these things together— stir well and drink fast.

grape juice, vinegar, mustard mayonnaise, juice from one lemon, pepper and salt, ketchup, olive oil, and a speck of onion.

P.S. The faster you drink it faster you get F·R·E·C·K·L·E·S

Andrew read the list twice. It didn't sound like much of a secret recipe. Well, he'd paid fifty cents. He might as well find out, and he only had an hour before his mother would be home.

MAYONNAI
MUSTA

Andrew climbed up on the kitchen counter so he could reach the cabinets. He found everything except the lemon—that was in the refrigerator—and the onion. Mrs. Marcus kept onions in the basement in a bin. Andrew ran downstairs and selected a small one, since the recipe only called for a speck. With or without the skin, Andrew wondered.

He chose a big blue glass. He'd start with just one glassful and then drink another if he wanted more freckles. No point in overdoing it the first time.

Now first the grape juice, Andrew thought. He filled the glass halfway and added an ice cube. All drinks tasted better cold and he was sure this one would too.

Then he added the other ingredients one by one. He put in some vinegar, hot mustard, one spoonful of mayonnaise and plenty of pepper and salt. Then some ketchup. That was hard to pour. But what about the olive oil? His mother had vegetable oil but no olive oil. Maybe the stuff that looked like water in the olive jar was what Sharon meant. He put in a few spoonfuls of that. Now for the lemon. Andrew cut one in half and squeezed. Now all he needed was that speck of onion and

he was all set. He stirred up the drink and smelled it.

OH! IT SMELLED AWFUL! JUST PLAIN AWFUL! He'd have to hold his nose when he drank it. He stuck his tongue into the glass to taste it. Ick! *Terrible!* He didn't know how he'd ever manage to get it down . . . and fast too. It said to drink very fast. That old Sharon! She probably thought he wouldn't be able to drink it. Well, he'd show her. He'd drink it all right!

Andrew held his nose, tilted his head back and gulped down Sharon's secret recipe for freckle juice. He felt like throwing up

. . . it was that bad! But if he did he'd never get freckles. No, he would be strong!

Andrew crept into his mother's bedroom. He didn't feel well enough to walk. He sat on the floor in front of the full-length mirror. He waited for something to happen.

Andrew won't give up easily in his search for freckles! Find out what happens by reading the rest of Freckle Juice.

Why Does My Shadow Change Size?

Have you ever taken a walk outdoors early in the morning and noticed that your shadow looks tall and skinny? And then later that day, did you notice that your shadow looks much shorter? Your shadow around noon is so short that you can probably stretch your leg over its head. Why do you suppose your shadow grows and shrinks in a day while you stay exactly the same size? And what is a shadow in the first place?

You make a shadow when your body gets in the way of shining light. The shadow is the dark patch that shows up when the light can't get through. Changing shadow size has to do with the sun's position in the sky. When the sun is low in the sky, close to the horizon (that's the line where the sky and the earth seem to meet), the sun is shining from the side, at an angle. It is not shining straight down like a flashlight would. This sideways angle of light is what makes your shadow tall and skinny or short and fat.

When the sun first comes up over the horizon in the morning, it is very low in the sky. The sun's light is coming toward your

body at a wide angle and so most of your body blocks the light. Therefore, your shadow is very tall. As the morning continues and the sun seems to move higher in the sky, the angle of light becomes smaller, and your shadow becomes shorter. By noon, the sun is high in the sky, like a ceiling light, and there is hardly any angle of light at all. It almost forms a straight line with your body, and your body is blocking

It's morning now.
The sun is still low
in the sky, and
shadows are long.

very little light from the sun. This makes a very short shadow.

As afternoon passes, the sun's position continues to move across the other side of the sky. As the sun moves downward, your shadow begins to grow taller again. By the time the sun is ready to set in the evening, it is very low in the sky, and your shadow will, once again, be very tall.

You can see for yourself how this works by using a flashlight, pretending it is the sun. Place a tall object, such as a vase or a toy figure, on the floor. Shine the flashlight as if it were the sun: first from one side, moving it upward until it is shining straight down, and then back down on the other side. Do you see how the shadow changes from tall to short to tall again? This is exactly what happens to your shadow outdoors as the day moves from morning to afternoon to evening.

Perhaps during all this shadow gazing you notice that not only your shadow's size changes, but its position changes, too. If you see your shadow on one side of you in the morning, it will be on the opposite side of you in the afternoon. That's because your shadow always falls on the side of you that is opposite where the sun's light is coming from. Your body is stopping the sun's light from getting to the ground. It's as if the sun's rays hit you and you fall down—away from the sun. Only it's not you that falls, it's your shadow—that changing patch of darkness you make by getting in the sun's way!

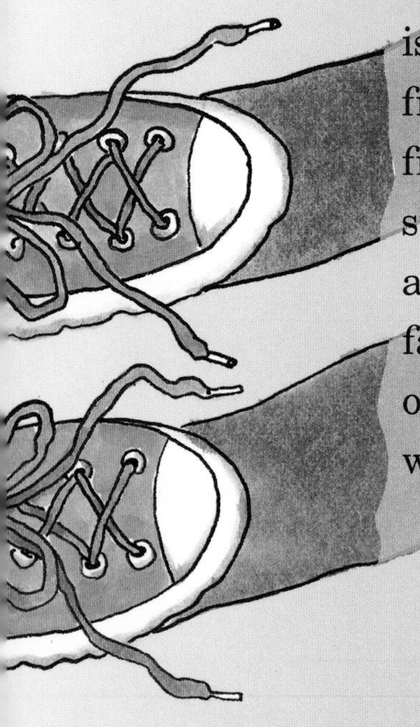

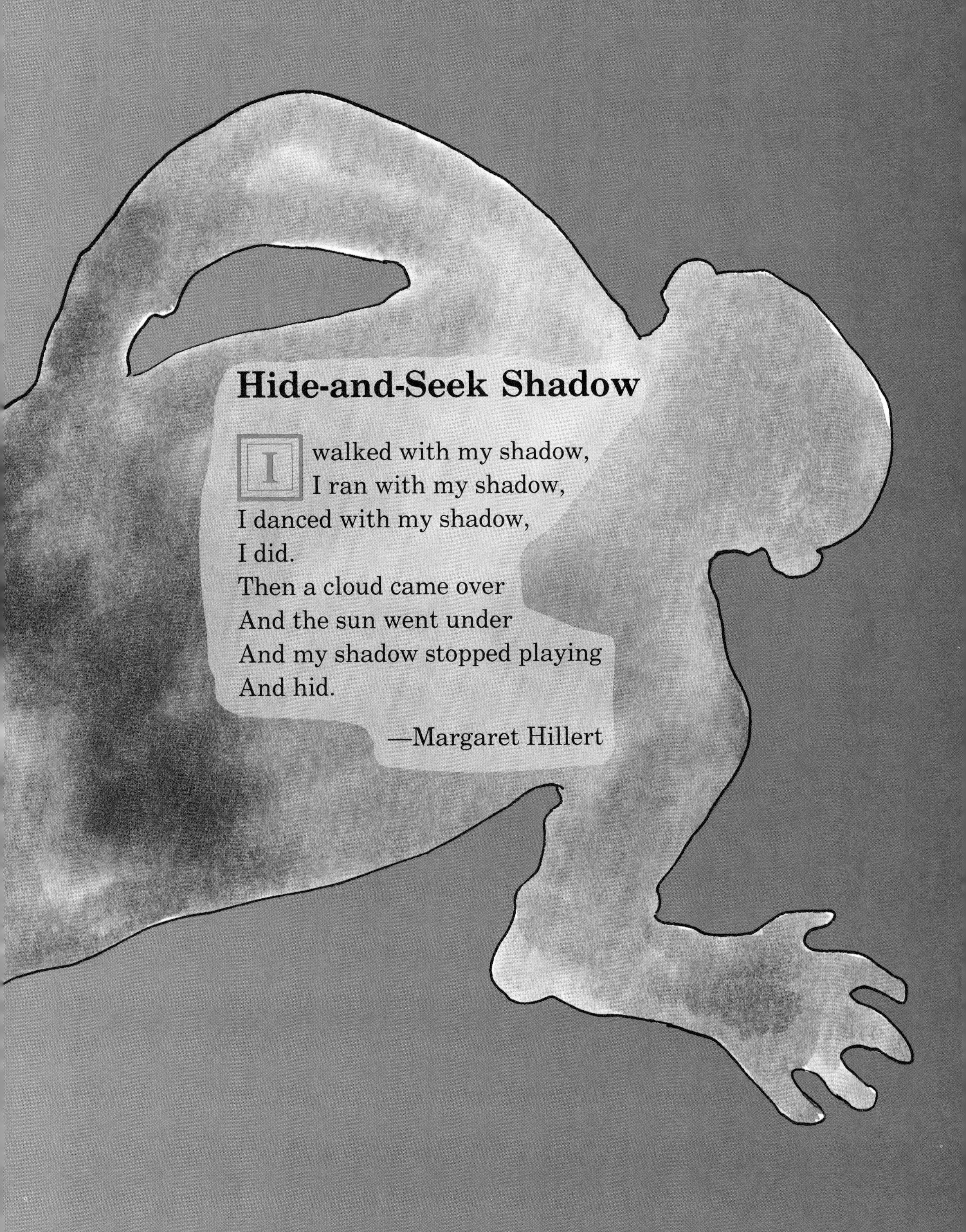

Hide-and-Seek Shadow

I walked with my shadow,
I ran with my shadow,
I danced with my shadow,
I did.
Then a cloud came over
And the sun went under
And my shadow stopped playing
And hid.

—Margaret Hillert

How do shadows change?

Things you need:
flashlight
cardboard
scissors
glue
Popsicle sticks

1. Cut different shapes out of cardboard and glue each of them to a Popsicle stick.

2. Shine a flashlight on a wall in a dark room.

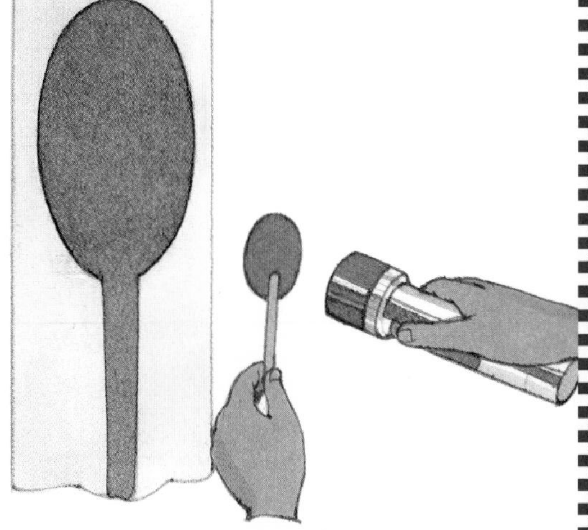

3. Hold the shape close to the flashlight. The shadow will look large on the wall because the shape is blocking out a lot of light.

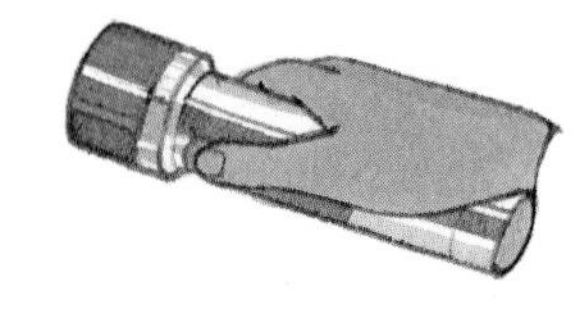

4. Place the shape farther from the flashlight. Does the shadow look different? It will look smaller because the shape is blocking out less light.

*Get permission first.

Why Does Hair Keep Growing?

Do you remember the story of Rapunzel? She was the beautiful maiden with hair so long she let it out the window of a tall tower so that the handsome prince could climb up to see her. And then the wicked witch found out and cut off Rapunzel's golden tresses. Drat! Never again would Rapunzel have hair so long. Or would she? Do you suppose Rapunzel's hair ever grew back?

Well, if the story were true, yes, her hair would grow back, at least to a point. It would take a while, though. Our hair usually grows just under six inches (15 centimeters) a year, and the tower in the story was probably 75 feet (22.5 meters) high!

Did you ever wonder why our hair keeps growing, even after we cut it? Cut off a pair of jeans and they won't grow back. "But jeans aren't alive," you might say. Did you know that the hair on your head is not alive

Straight, curly, and wavy: hair comes in many forms.

either? It is really made up of dead hair cells. How then can it grow?

Your hair does not grow from the very end where it was last cut. Rather, it grows from underneath your scalp. You have tiny openings in your scalp from which hair grows—about 100,000, to be exact. These openings are called follicles (FAWL ih kuhlz). The part of each hair at the bottom of the follicle, deep under your scalp, is the root. New hair cells are always being formed at the root, and they push the "old" cells up and away from the nourishment that is near the root. Without nourishment, the hair cells turn to a hard protein substance called keratin (KEH ruh tihn), which is what your

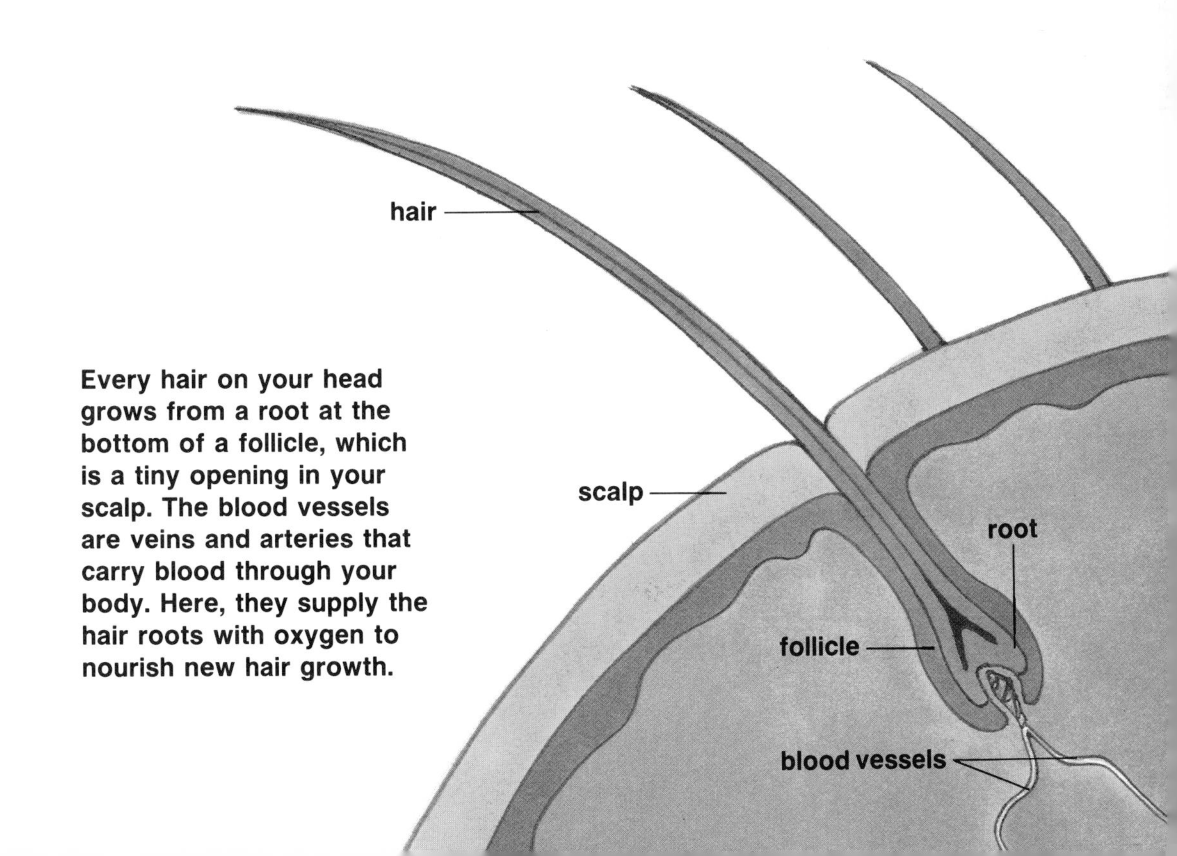

Every hair on your head grows from a root at the bottom of a follicle, which is a tiny opening in your scalp. The blood vessels are veins and arteries that carry blood through your body. Here, they supply the hair roots with oxygen to nourish new hair growth.

hair is made of. This "old" hair is soon pushed up and out of your scalp. Your hair keeps getting longer until you cut it or your hair follicles take a rest.

Each hair on your head keeps growing for anywhere from two to six years. Then each hair follicle takes a rest for a few months and stops making new hair cells, but not all at the same time. They take turns. Those hairs from the resting follicles soon break off and fall out, usually when you're combing or brushing your hair. You can lose up to 100 hairs each day, but you'll hardly notice. The follicles soon begin making new hair cells again.

Using a little math, you can figure out that if hair grows nearly six inches (15 centimeters) a year and can grow for six years, if you don't cut it, it might grow to be about 36 inches (90 centimeters). But it probably won't ever grow much longer than that. Sorry, Rapunzel!

I Wonder What This Is.

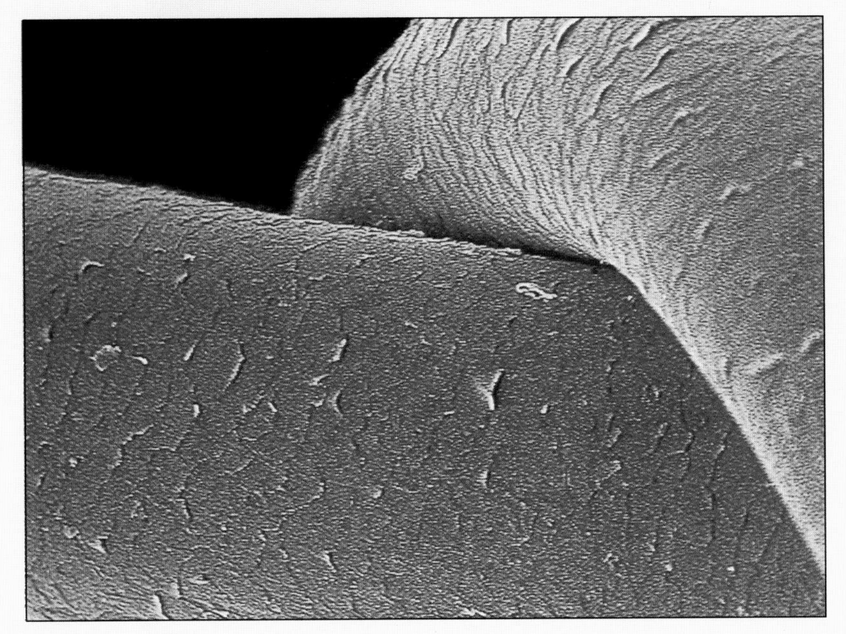

Clue: They come in many colors and styles, and you see them every day.

Find the answer on page 242.

Simple Science*

How does moisture change your hair?

Things you need:
ruler
tape
1 to 3 hairs, long enough to handle easily
warm water
glass or sink

1. Tape the hairs to one end of the ruler.

2. Press down over the tape with your thumb and tug the hairs gently. Note how long the hairs are.

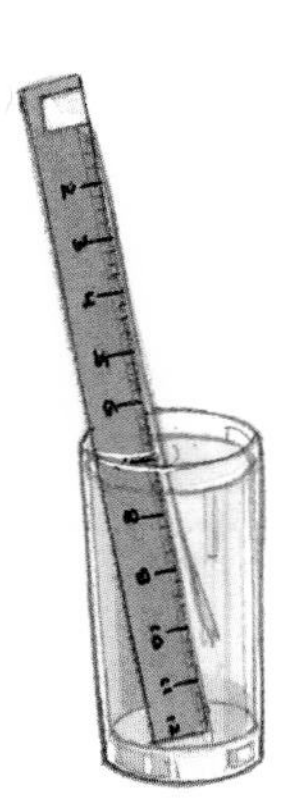

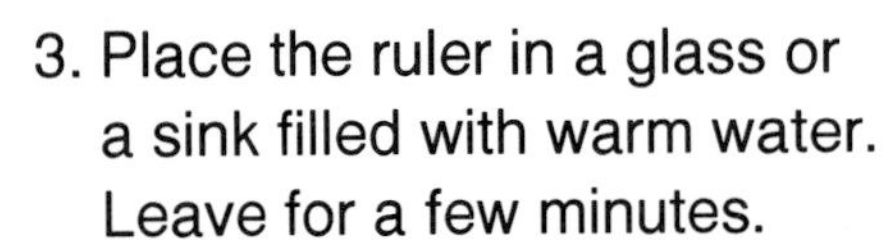

3. Place the ruler in a glass or a sink filled with warm water. Leave for a few minutes.

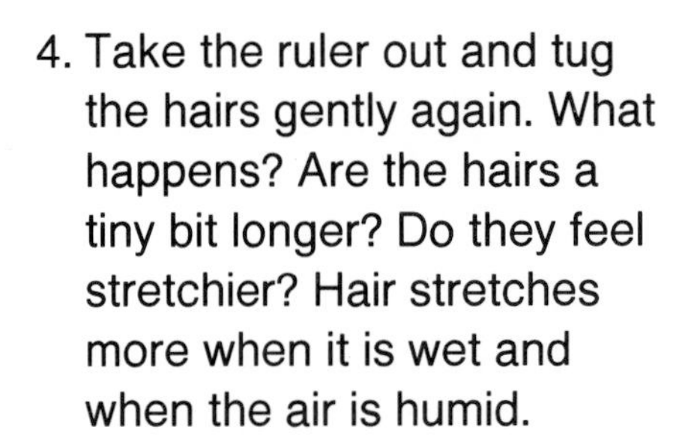

4. Take the ruler out and tug the hairs gently again. What happens? Are the hairs a tiny bit longer? Do they feel stretchier? Hair stretches more when it is wet and when the air is humid.

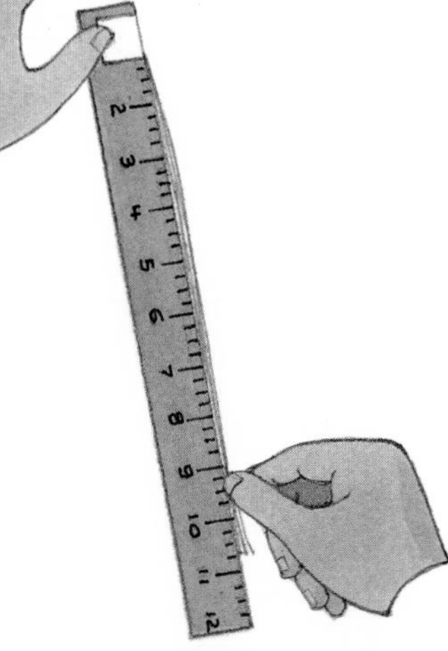

*Get permission first.

Keep On Dreaming— Why Do We Do It?

"What a dream I had last night!" Sue told her friends when she got to school. "I dreamed I was a TV news reporter covering an important story at the White House. I was talking to the President, and he even knew my name."

"I never dream," complained Josie.

"I dream every night," said Rosie.

"I dream once in a while," replied Ray.

Josie, Rosie, and Ray don't know it, but all three of them, as well as everyone else, dream every night, usually about three to five times. But many of us don't remember what we dream, or even that we've dreamed at all. We only remember the dream we were having when we woke up. Sometimes we might remember that we dreamed, but we can't remember what our dreams were about. Other times we might remember a dream very clearly as if it really happened. Sometimes a dream is so pleasant that we

Even a very exciting show you saw on television could pop up again in your dreams.

wish we could go back to sleep to finish the dream.

There are bad dreams, too. They're called nightmares. Have you ever awoke crying or yelling because you were frightened by a dragon or something else chasing you in your dreams? A nightmare can be very scary. Where do these dreams come from, and why do we have them? Have you wondered about this?

Dreams come in all shapes and sizes. They can be long or short, silly or sad, wild or tame, or just plain weird. You never

know what you are going to dream about. But most of the time you will dream about things that happened to you or things you thought about during the day. Each day your brain tucks away all sorts of information, even things that you hardly noticed—maybe an old woman you glimpsed from the school bus picking flowers in her garden. And then you'll wonder why you dreamed that you were an old woman picking flowers. There are many scenes during your busy day that you don't have time to even think about. Any one of these may pop up in your dreams.

During the night, your body sleeps, but your brain keeps working. It may rest awhile and then start thinking about that woman you hardly noticed. That's one dream. Then your brain will rest again and soon think some more. This time, maybe it will think about something that has been worrying you, maybe a math quiz. This brainwork continues all through the night. The brain is always pulling bits of information out of its file cabinet to think about, things you didn't even know it filed away.

Things that happen while you sleep might cause a dream. If your blanket slips

"Hmmm, a loud noise. I must be in a rocket ship."

off and you get cold, you might dream you are a famous Arctic explorer. If you hear an airplane while you sleep, you might dream about a huge, noisy rocket ship. Your brain is truly amazing.

Back in the classroom, Sue was handed her report on the White House. "Nice job, Susan," Ms. Kaufman said.

Can you guess what caused Sue's dream last night?

Down to Earth Wonders

Why Can't We Feel the Earth Spin?

Hold on! Right this minute, the earth beneath you is spinning like a top. A person standing at the equator is moving at over 1,000 miles (1,600 kilometers) an hour. That's faster than a 747 jet!

This spinning causes day and night. It is daytime when our side of the earth is facing the sun. Night comes when our side of the earth is turned away from the sun.

The earth is not only spinning. It is also moving in a very big circle around the sun. The earth takes about 365 days, or one year, to make a full trip around the sun. It is going at the speed of about 65,600 miles (104,960 kilometers) an hour. That's much faster than a rocket!

Have you ever wondered why we can't feel the earth move? And with all this spinning and circling, you would think we earth people would be pretty dizzy. Yet, most of the time, we don't think about the earth moving at all. To us, it seems like the earth is standing still. When we look at the sky, it's the sun and stars that seem to be moving, not the earth. And even the sun and stars don't seem to be moving by very fast.

But back to our question—why can't we feel the earth move? One reason is that the earth moves smoothly and constantly. It never stops. It always goes at the same speed.

Think about when you ride in a car. How do you know the car is moving? You hear the motor running. You hear the car hum. Through the car window, you see that houses and trees seem to move past you. Air rushes into the window and blows on your face. You feel the car go over bumps in the road. When the car speeds up, your body feels pressed against the seat. When the car stops suddenly, your head may jerk forward.

As you can see, a car gives you many signs to tell you it is moving. The earth does not give you so many signs. Since it is not

a machine, the earth does not make noise or jiggle when it moves. The earth moves in space. So it has nothing to roll over or rub up against.

The air that surrounds our earth moves along with it. The earth's movement doesn't blast wind in our faces. The earth always moves at the same speed. So we never feel any slowing down or speeding up.

But just as we see trees and houses go by as we ride in a car, we *do see* the sun and stars go by as the earth spins. The stars also change places in the sky as the earth moves around the sun.

True, the sun and stars don't seem to be moving by very fast. That's because they are so far away. When you are in a moving car, close things, like the road beneath you, seem to rush by in a blur. But faraway things, like a mountain in the distance, hardly seem to move at all.

We are used to the earth's movement. In a way, we are like fish. A fish cannot "feel" wet because it has never known what it's like to be dry. We cannot feel the earth moving because we have never known what it's like to have the world *not* move.

I Wonder What This Is.

Clue: Life wouldn't be the same anywhere else.
Find the answer on page 242.

Why Do Days Get Longer and Shorter?

Astronaut Andrews here. During my last space voyage, I did a lot of earth watching. Maybe I can shed some light on your question.

From space, I could see that the sun never moves. It beams like a great, ever-burning flashlight. This light is in a circle that always covers one-half of the earth. But that half is always moving. The earth keeps shifting under the sun's circle of daylight.

The shifting comes about partly because the earth is tilted constantly at an angle. This tilt helps give a different amount of daylight to the different parts of the world.

Can you find the Northern Hemisphere in the globe below?

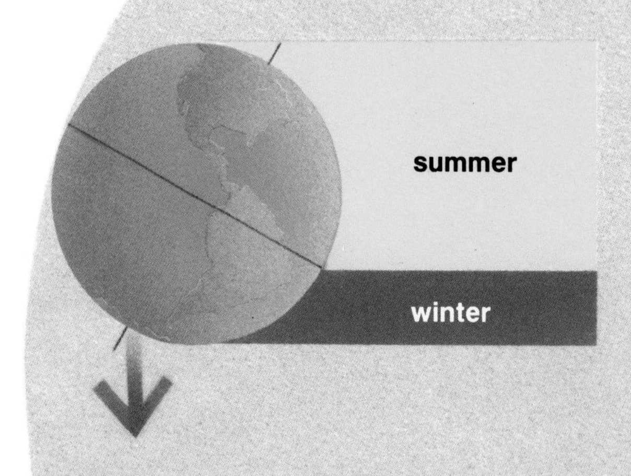

Where do you live and what time of year is it? These facts have a lot to do with how much daylight you get.

On June 21 or June 22, the Northern Hemisphere, or "top half" of the earth, is tilted toward the sun. So the Northern Hemisphere gets more of the sun's rays than the Southern Hemisphere, or "bottom half" of the earth. In other words, days are longest at this time of year.

If you live in the United States, you enjoy long days at this time of year. If you live near Point Barrow, Alaska, you can look

Why do you think days are colder and shorter in the Northern Hemisphere now (below)?

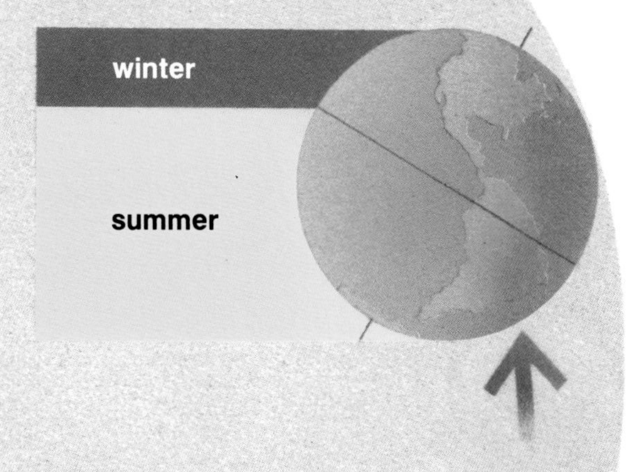

forward to several weeks of round-the-clock daylight. That's because the tilt of the earth places the whole Arctic Circle within reach of the sun's rays for the whole twenty-four hours that the earth takes to spin around, or rotate.

At the same time, people in the Southern Hemisphere have the shortest days of their year—their winter. And the Antarctic Circle stays dark for weeks.

As the year moves on, the earth keeps circling the sun. Fewer and fewer places in the Arctic have constant daylight now. Then

An Arctic summer day . . .

the Northern Hemisphere is no longer tilted toward the sun. By September 22 or 23, both hemispheres get an equal amount of the sun's rays. Fall begins in the Northern Hemisphere, and spring begins in the Southern Hemisphere.

On December 21 or 22, the Southern Hemisphere is tilted toward the sun. Now that half of the earth enjoys the long days. The Antarctic has weeks of daylight. The Northern Hemisphere has its shortest days, and the Arctic has weeks of darkness.

What happens in September also happens on March 20 or 21. Both hemispheres get an equal amount of the sun's rays. During spring and fall, the days and nights all over the earth are about equal. However, the

and the sun never sets!

days near the poles seem shorter than those nearer the equator. The reason is the angle of the sun's rays.

The equator receives the sun's most direct rays. In Hawaii and other places near the equator, the sun seems directly overhead all day long. It shines bright and warm almost until sunset.

Places near the poles receive more slanted rays from the sun. As a result, the sun hangs low in the horizon hours before sunset. So in northern Canada and other places near the poles, twilight seems to come early and to linger. That's the sun for you: a little light here, a lot there. Daylight may be shifting around, but the sun is always shining somewhere on earth.

Maui Tames the Sun

A folk tale from the Pacific Islands

Maui was especially good at playing tricks and not being found when there was work to be done. That's how he earned the reputation of mischief-maker and prankster. Some people thought that Maui was lazy. They knew that there was nothing he loved more than to bask in the warmth of the sun. Others thought that Maui earned his leisure. Gather round for a tale. Then, decide for yourself.

Long ago when the earth was young, the sun soared across the sky at an alarming speed. It soared through the sky so quickly that no matter how early people rose for work, before they could finish what needed to be done, darkness fell. Farmers never had enough daylight to plant their fields. Fishers could not catch fish. Weavers could not weave cloth. All were frustrated. Day was done before the villagers could fulfill their duties. No one thought that there was anything they could do—that is, no one except Maui.

One evening, Maui's brothers were sitting around the fire discussing the matter. Maui jumped up. "I can tame the sun! I have a plan, but I will need your help." Maui's brothers argued that it was not possible. They said that the sun would burn him to a crisp. But Maui would not back down. At last, if only to prove him wrong, his brothers agreed to help.

Maui ordered his brothers to make a net out of coconut fibers. They braided one. It was so strong that even the brothers began to believe it would hold the sun. Eagerly, they dragged the mighty net to the edge of the horizon. They approached the cave where the sun hides at night. Silently, they strung the net across the mouth of the cave. The sun blasted out of the cave. The brothers watched. But the net tore as if it were a spider's web.

Maui was not discouraged. He had another trick up his sleeve. "Weave a net out of coconut rope. Make it as thick as a tree," he told his brothers. They wove such a net and spread it across the cave.

This time, when the sun burst forth, it was indeed caught in the net. Maui and his brothers struggled to hold the sun. But, it thrashed wildly. In a flash, the net burst into flames. Freed, the sun shot off once again across the sky.

Maui spoke again, “I have a better idea.” This time he went off to see his mother. For Maui knew that she could help with her magic hair. His mother listened carefully to his idea and agreed to help. And what did she do next but cut off her hair and weave a net out of it! Then she gave the net to

Maui, who rushed back to his brothers. The brothers carefully hung the new net across the cave, and they waited. Out zoomed the sun after a while. Thwhack! Now it was captured.

Maui shouted to the sun, "I will set you free if you promise to fly across the sky slowly. We need more hours in a day than you give us." The thrashing, swirling giant sun agreed to slow down.

The next morning, the sun rose in the sky, and Maui's brothers awoke saying, "We'd best get started before day ends."

"No hurry," said the trusting Maui. He stretched out on the soft sand in the warm sun. All day long, he remained. When at last the sun did set many hours later, Maui saw the tangled strands of the hair. They were streaming off the sun into the sea. "Amazing to behold," thought Maui. "Amazing to have time to notice."

Maui indeed tamed the sun, for as you see, the sun still keeps its promise. That is why we have time for work, play, and rest during a day.

What Good Is Dirt?

Sometimes dirt seems like just a pain in the neck. If it weren't for dirt, your mom would never have to tell you, "Clean those dirty hands!" or "Wipe those dirty feet!"

Why do we have dirt anyway, if we have to keep washing it off our hands? Wouldn't the world be better off without it?

The truth is, we couldn't live without dirt—officially called soil. Soil makes plants grow. If there were no soil, there would be no plants. Without plants, we would have no food to eat.

Soil holds the roots of plants in the ground. It holds water in the ground, too, so that the roots can drink. Soil even gives plants their favorite food, minerals. These are those nonliving materials found in the earth. Minerals come from the ground-up

rocks in soil. Now, that may not sound yummy *to you*. But to a plant, minerals are better than peanut butter sandwiches. A mineral called potassium (puh TAS ee uhm) helps plants grow.

Besides helping plants grow, soil is the home of many living things. Most likely, you have seen the little animals that live in soil, such as ants, beetles, and worms. And you know about the bigger animals that make their homes in the ground, such as snakes, gophers, and moles.

But do you know what the most important living things in soil are? They are the ones you can't see at all. In one spoonful of soil live millions of microorganisms. Microorganisms are plants and animals that you can't see without a microscope.

The microorganisms in soil make things rot. This is an important job. Imagine what life would be like if nothing ever rotted away! Dead birds would fall to the ground and just stay there forever. The leaves that fall from the trees would keep piling up each year until they buried us.

The microorganisms in dirt eat up dead plants and animals, eggshells and apple cores. They turn this "garbage" into matter that plants can use for food.

Have you ever heard someone say, "It's as worthless as dirt"? Don't believe it. Dirt is worth a lot. It makes plants grow. The microorganisms living in it make things rot. Without dirt, life on earth would come to a dead stop.

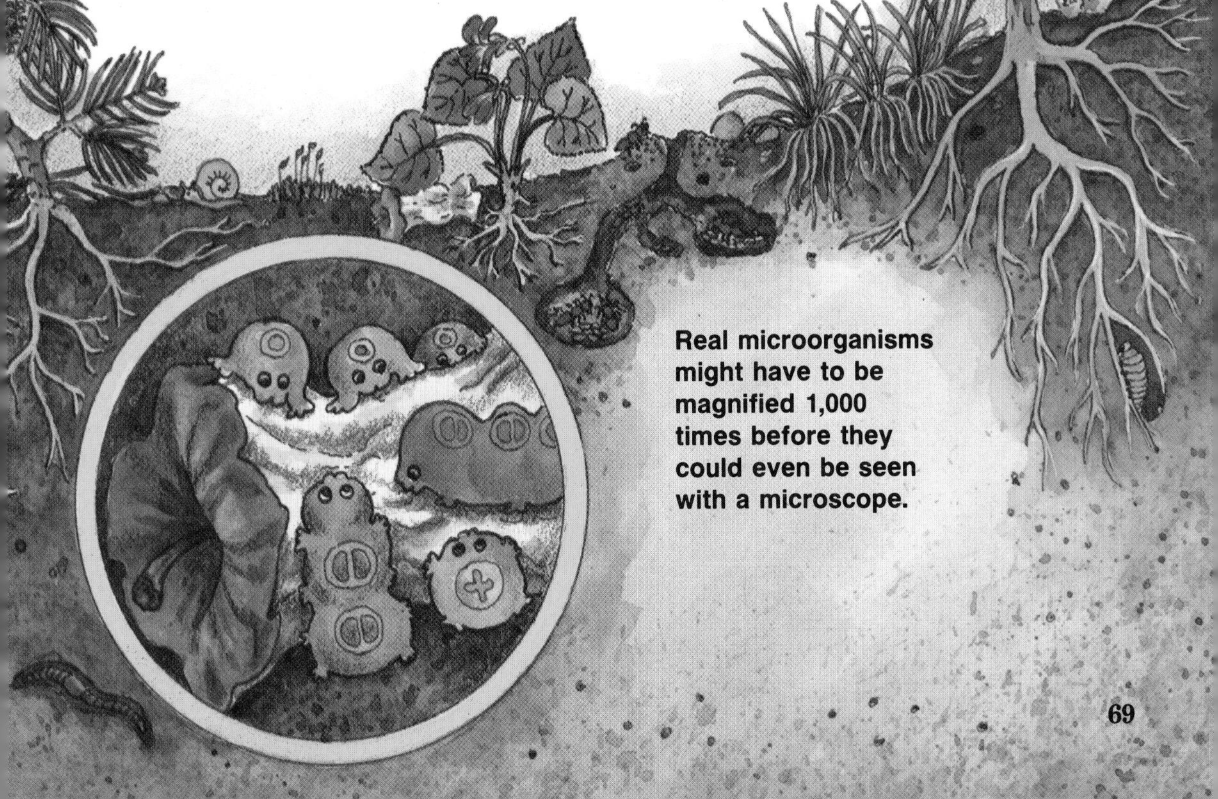

Real microorganisms might have to be magnified 1,000 times before they could even be seen with a microscope.

How Did Soil Form?

Has the dirt, we mean the soil, in your backyard always been there? Or did it come from someplace else? How is soil made in the first place?

All soil begins as rock. Once upon a time, the dirt in your backyard could have been a piece of mountain. The sun beat down on the mountain every day and then the rock cooled off at night. All that temperature change made the rock crack.

Then rain poured down on the rock, washing away tiny bits of it. After a while, a chunk of rock broke off and tumbled down the mountain. It may have fallen into a river. There, the rushing water hit it against

other rocks. Or, if it fell on a field, the wind blew grains of sand against it.

The rock may even have fallen beside a glacier (GLAY shur). A glacier is a huge, slow-moving river of ice. A glacier crushes the rocks beneath it and carries them away.

If the rock ended up in a sunny, wet place, a fuzzy growth known as lichens (LY kuhnz) may have formed on it. Lichens make acids that help dissolve rock. Plants may have helped break up the rock by poking it with their roots.

Sun, wind, rain, ice, rivers, glaciers, and plants—all of them worked together to grind a piece of rock. It was no easy job! It takes hundreds of years to make a spoonful of soil that covers your yard.

Water and blowing sand blast away at rock, loosening it into soil. Below, velvety lichens grow on rock, helping to break it down into soil, too.

What Happens If You Keep on Digging?

Have you ever tried digging a hole just to see how far down you could go? Do you think you could reach China, maybe? Let's find out. It's easy to dig at first, where the soft topsoil is. Topsoil is loose dirt with worms and bugs and plant roots in it.

After the topsoil, though, you would find wet clay or sand or gravel. This stuff is harder to dig through.

If you could keep on digging, eventually you would hit bedrock. This is the rock that makes up the earth's crust. The crust is

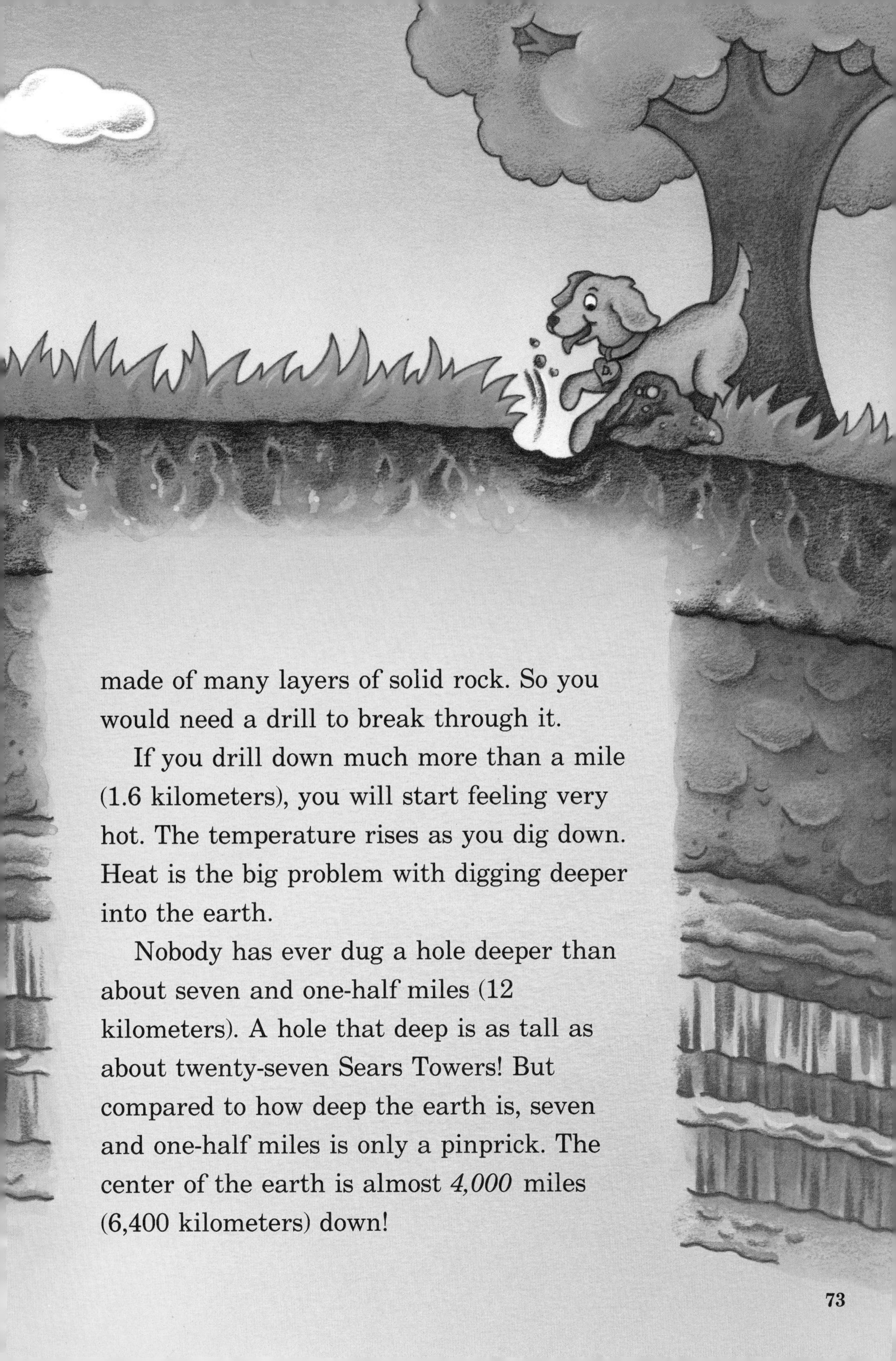

made of many layers of solid rock. So you would need a drill to break through it.

If you drill down much more than a mile (1.6 kilometers), you will start feeling very hot. The temperature rises as you dig down. Heat is the big problem with digging deeper into the earth.

Nobody has ever dug a hole deeper than about seven and one-half miles (12 kilometers). A hole that deep is as tall as about twenty-seven Sears Towers! But compared to how deep the earth is, seven and one-half miles is only a pinprick. The center of the earth is almost *4,000* miles (6,400 kilometers) down!

INNER CORE
OUTER CORE
MANTLE
CRUST
HOT

Suppose, just suppose, you could dig deep into the earth without being burned by the heat. After the crust, you would come to the mantle. The mantle is about 1,800 miles (2,880 kilometers) thick. The first part of the mantle is solid and joined with the crust, but scientists believe that parts of it are soft. It gets very hot—parts of it may reach over 7000 °F (3871 °C). That's much hotter than a house on fire! You might find areas of magma (MAG muh), the hot, glowing melted rock that spurts out of volcanoes.

After tunneling through the mantle, you would drop into a hot yellow soup made up mostly of the melted metals nickel and iron. You would have to swim through this liquid outer core of the earth for about 1,400 miles (2,240 kilometers).

Then you would come to the earth's inner core. This is a solid ball, mainly of iron and nickel, that glows white hot. It is almost as big as the moon!

If you drilled about 800 more miles (1,280 kilometers) into the inner core, you'd be at the center of the earth. Here is the hottest place in earth—perhaps as high as 9000 °F (4982 °C).

At the center of the earth, you would feel squashed. The weight of the whole world would press on you from all sides! So you would not stay there long.

If you kept drilling, sooner or later you would come out on the other side of the earth. Suppose you started your hole in the United States. Then you would come out at the bottom of the Indian Ocean. It's not China, but it is a nice, cool end to a long, hot trip!

A mountainside may look like ripples of rock.

Mighty Mountains: Why Are You Here?

You want to know why the Rockies and our other mountains are here? Of all the crust! But I'll tell you anyway:

Over millions of years, many layers of sediment—bits of rock, clay, and tiny animal bones—built up on the earth's crust. Remember the crust? It's that layer of rock surrounding the surface of the earth. Beneath the ocean, the crust is mostly made of a heavy rock called basalt (buh SAWLT).

The crust beneath the continents is thicker. It has a bottom layer of basalt and another layer of a lighter rock that is called granite (GRAN iht).

But let's get back to the sediment. Each layer of sediment on the crust pressed down on the layers below it. Over time, this pressure helped harden the sediment into a rock we call sedimentary rock. The Rockies are mostly granite and sedimentary rock. Now the rock was here long before the mountains. To form mountains, the earth's crust had to move!

Scientists believe that the crust is divided into huge sections called plates. Generally, each continent rests on its own plate. Other plates make up the ocean floor. The plates slide over the hot, soft rock in the mantle under the earth's crust.

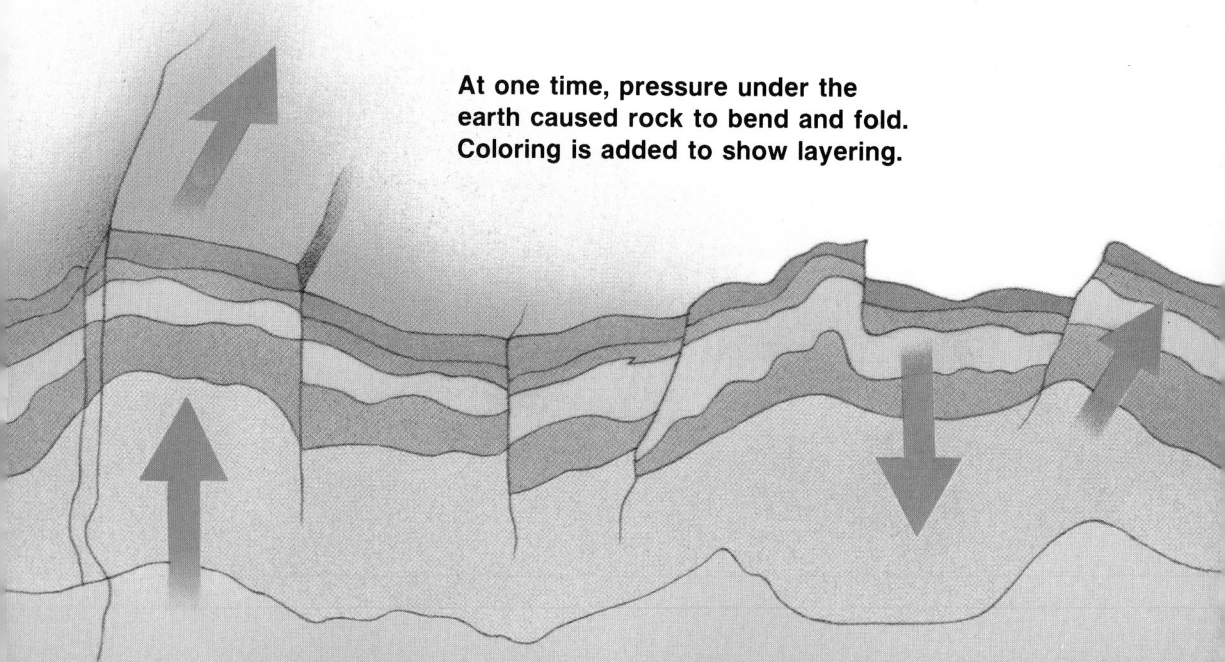

At one time, pressure under the earth caused rock to bend and fold. Coloring is added to show layering.

About 66 million years ago, the North American plate and the Pacific Ocean plate to its west collided. The pressure caused some rock to fold up into ridges. Some folded down into lower areas called troughs. And some mounded into domes. In this way, the Rockies were born. Imagine you could slice off a side of my slope and look at its cross section. You would find layer upon layer of wavelike folds in the sedimentary rock.

Not all mountains are like me, of course. Some mountains began with a fault rather than a fold. A fault is a crack in the earth's crust. In some cases, a block of rock lies between two faults. When a plate moves, the rock on either side of the block pushes on it

and may lift up the whole block. Or just one side of the block may tilt up. California's Sierra Nevadas are a tilted fault block.

Sometimes a plate movement lifts up a flat-topped block, creating a plateau (pla TOH). This is a large, raised section of land. Frost and plant roots may break up the sedimentary rock on the plateau. Then rain washes away the pieces. Wind may blast away even more rock. Eventually, frost, roots, rain, and wind carve ridges—sometimes called erosion (ih ROH zhuhn) mountains. *Erosion* means "wearing away." You can find erosion mountains in the Eastern United States.

Folded, fault block, and erosion mountains form over millions of years. But volcanoes form almost instantly. *Volcano* can mean an opening in the crust that oozes lava—hot liquid rock. It also can mean the mountain formed after the lava cools and hardens. Volcanoes are really a story in themselves, though. Just read on!

Why Are Some Mountains Always Snow-Capped?

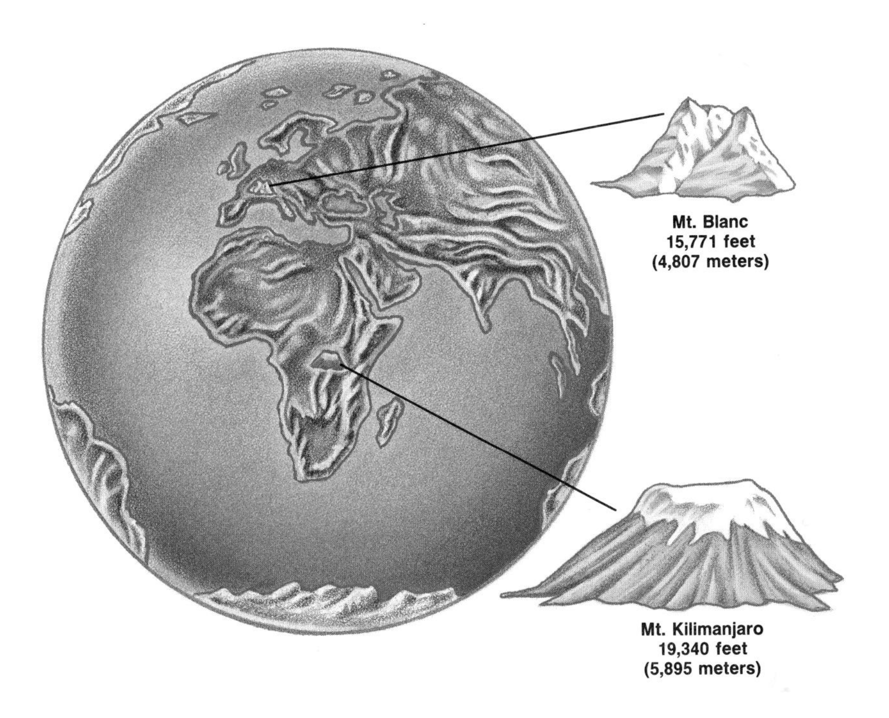

On the hottest summer day you can look up at some of the tallest mountains and still see snow. How come? For snow to fall and to stay on a mountain peak, the temperature must stay close to 32 °F (0 °C). The higher up the mountain, the colder it is compared to the ground below. But keep in mind that ground temperatures vary, and it's always warmer near the equator. A mountain in a warm region would have to be taller to keep a snowcap all year. The snowcap on Mount Kilimanjaro (kihl uh muhn JAHR oh) in Africa, near the equator, starts at 15,000 feet (4,572 meters) above sea level. The snowcaps on the Alps farther north begin at 8,500 feet (2,591 meters).

Why Do Volcanoes Erupt?

How can a mountain form instantly? How can a section of earth just burst open? In other words, what causes volcanoes? The answer has to do with what's going on inside the earth.

If you took the trip inside the earth (pages 72-76), you'll remember that it is very hot deep inside. What does this have to do with volcanoes? The hot temperatures melt the rock into magma. Also, the heat changes some of the rock into gases. The gas makes the magma lighter than the rock around it, and the magma rises toward the surface. Near the surface, the gases quickly expand, which means they fill up more space.

Some of this rising magma can burst through openings in the earth's crust. In other words, a volcano erupts (ih RUHPTZ). The magma is called

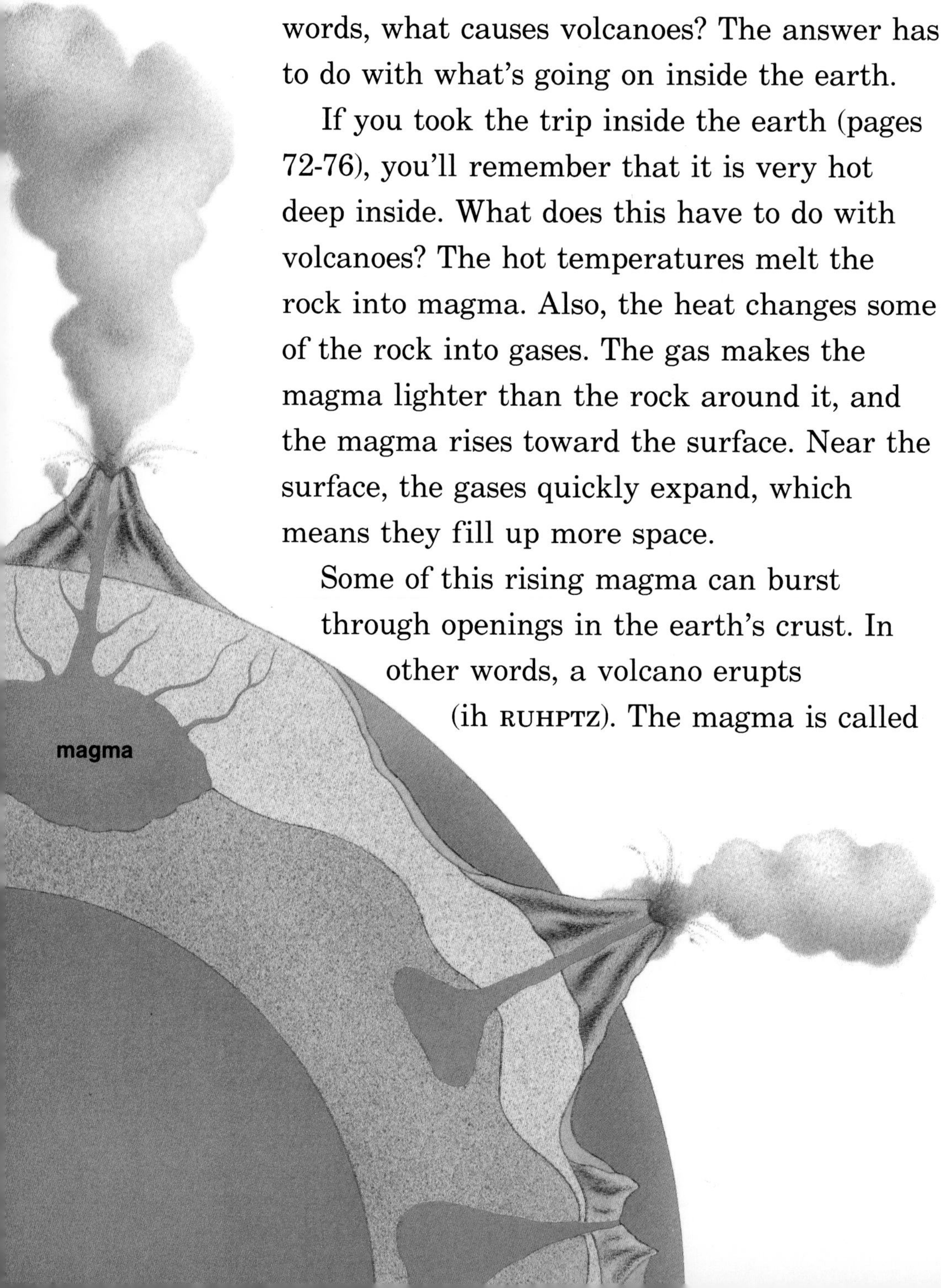

magma

Lava rushes down Mount Etna in Italy. This famous volcano has erupted at least 260 times!

lava when it bursts through the earth's surface. Flowing lava and other materials blasted out of the earth during a volcanic eruption can create a mountain.

Why do we have volcanoes in some places and not in others? The answer is in the plates. Remember those huge sections of earth's crust that rest on the mantle? A map of the world's volcanoes shows that many form where two plates meet and collide. In fact, you'll find most volcanoes near the boundaries of the Pacific plate. This belt around the rim of the Pacific is called the "Ring of Fire."

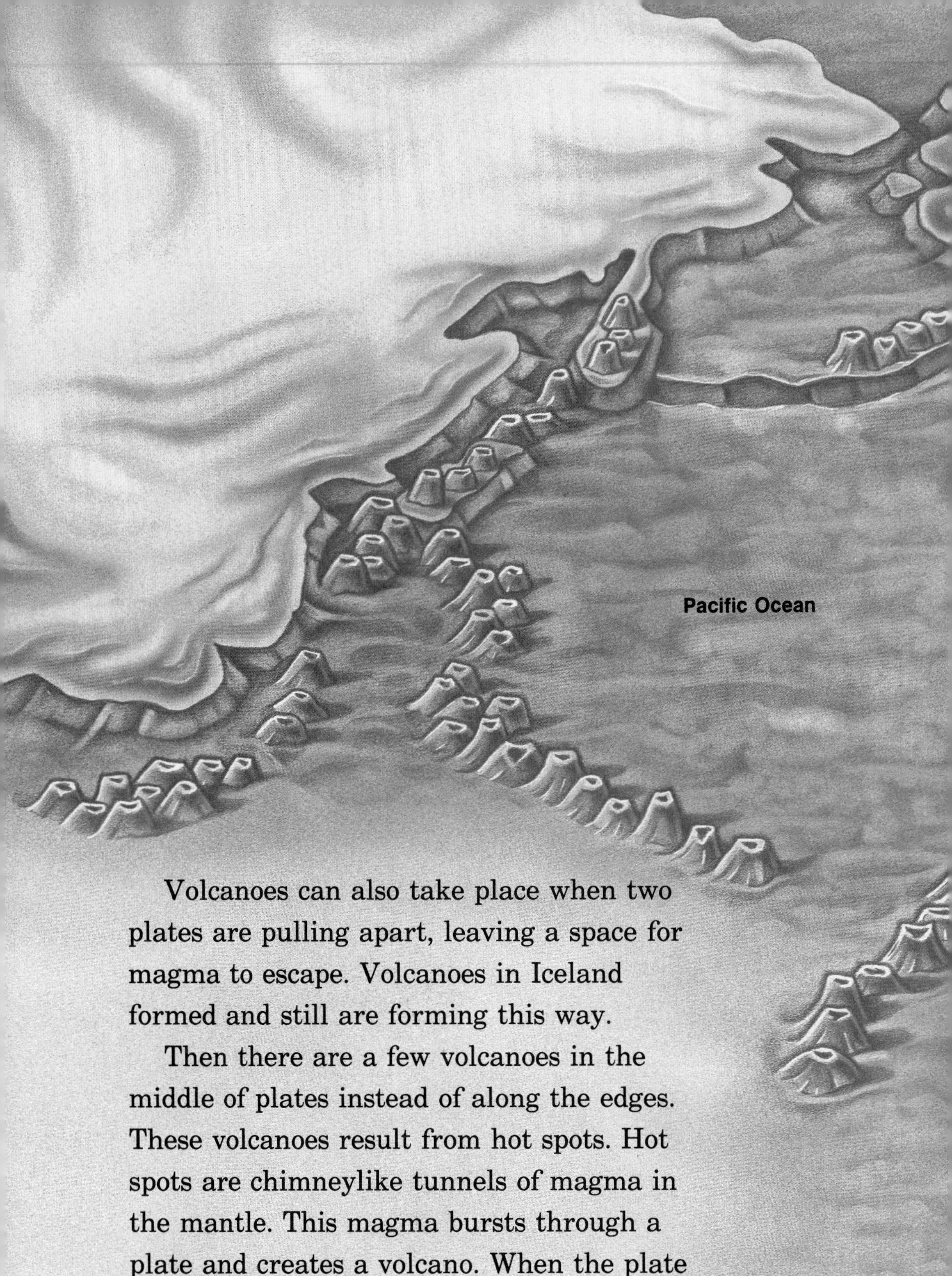

Volcanoes can also take place when two plates are pulling apart, leaving a space for magma to escape. Volcanoes in Iceland formed and still are forming this way.

Then there are a few volcanoes in the middle of plates instead of along the edges. These volcanoes result from hot spots. Hot spots are chimneylike tunnels of magma in the mantle. This magma bursts through a plate and creates a volcano. When the plate moves, it carries the volcano with it. But the hot spot stays put and may make a new volcano behind the old one. Over millions of years, a chain of volcanoes may form. The Hawaiian Islands, which are volcanic mountains, formed this way.

And that is the story behind, or rather under, volcanoes. When you think of it, there really is a lot of action inside this quiet-looking earth of ours!

Hawaiian Island volcanoes

Mount Kiluea in Hawaii

Simple Science*

How does a volcano erupt?

Things you need
large box lid
newspaper
large, open-top can
sand
1/2 cup water
3/4 cup vinegar
2-3 drops red food coloring
1/4 cup baking soda
wooden stick

1. Place a thick padding of newspaper on the bottom of the box lid. (It's best to do this experiment outside.)

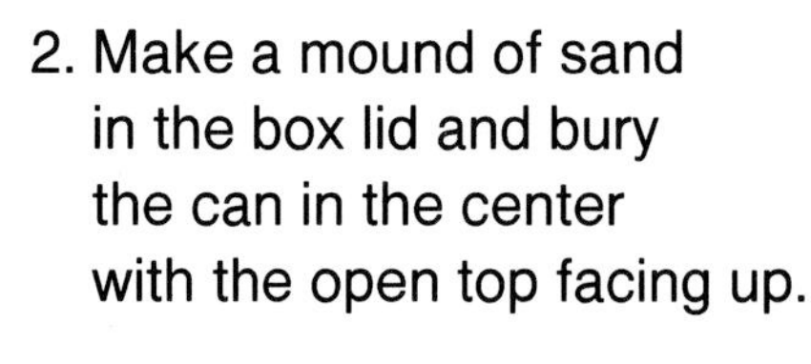

2. Make a mound of sand in the box lid and bury the can in the center with the open top facing up.

3. Pour the baking soda into the can. Then mix in the food coloring and water. Put the vinegar in last. What happens?

4. Your volcano is bubbling somewhat as gas-filled magma rushes up a real volcano. Here, the baking soda and vinegar release a gas.

*Get permission first.

Why Do We Have Earthquakes?

If mountains can erupt, what else can happen on this mysterious earth of ours? The earth can "quake," that's what. What is an earthquake and why does it happen?

We're back to the plates of the earth's crust again for the answer. Remember the story about mountains? The moving plates helped to build some mountains. At times, the slowly moving plates collide and cause rock to bend along the edges of plates and along those cracks called faults. Scientists believe that sometimes the bent rock snaps back like a harp string after a musician plucks it. And like the harp string, the rock vibrates. We call these vibrations an earthquake.

The vibrations, or shocks, of an earthquake travel through the earth in waves. They may move fast, like the coils of a spring when you stretch it and then let go. Other waves from an earthquake move more slowly. They move up and down or side to

The terrible work of earthquakes

El Salvador

side as they travel, like the ripple that moves along a rope when you snap it.

The shocks on the earth's surface are really the slowest waves of an earthquake. They travel in widening circles—like ripples in a pond—over the surface of the earth. These are the shocks that topple tall buildings. They cause most of the damage that comes with major earthquakes.

As many as a million earthquakes may take place on earth each year. A million

Algeria

Oakland, California

earthquakes? Actually, most of them take place under the ocean. That's one reason we don't feel them. Also, many earthquakes are not strong enough to do any damage.

What about the ones that people do feel? Some occur along faults on land. The San Andreas (SAN an DRAY uhs) Fault is the best known in North America. It runs about 600 miles (960 kilometers) from the Gulf of California to San Francisco. Many earthquakes along the San Andreas Fault hardly rattle the dishes in Californians' kitchens. But once in a while, the area around the San Andreas really shakes, as in October 1989, when highways and homes collapsed in San Francisco and nearby.

What about the underwater earthquakes? Most of them take place where underwater plates meet. These quakes can send waves speeding across thousands of ocean miles (kilometers). When the waves meet land, they become giant walls of water that crash down with driving force. And, of course, people would feel the effects of these earthquakes if their homes were near the shoreline on the waves' paths.

Shaking earth, colliding crust, raging waves? These result from earthquakes, planet earth's sometimes terrible wonders.

Sea Wave

It tumbled and it crumbled
Like a mountain in a quake.
It thundered and I wondered
At the power it could make.
It trickled and it tickled me.
I saw it disappear.
The mountain was a murmuring
Of ocean in my ear.

—Sandra Liatsos

Why Do Oceans and Lakes Have Waves?

Have you ever sat on a beach and watched the waves slap the shore? It looks like the water is trying to move farther onto the land. A wave rolls forward. But then it flattens and pulls back again. What causes waves? We know that underwater earthquakes can make the biggest waves of all. But what about regular waves? Winds cause most of these.

Wind blows across the top of water, causing ripples. Have you ever blown on a bowl of soup to cool it off? Then you have seen how blowing makes ripples. Once a

ripple is made, the wind has something to catch hold of. The wind can keep blowing on the ripple until it grows into a wave.

Ocean storms create the winds' greatest waves, and the biggest of the storm waves can be storm surges. The strong winds can blow the waves for long distances for several hours or more. Waves in small lakes can never get bigger than a few feet (meters).

On a beach, it may seem like water is traveling toward the land. Really, it's just the waves that are moving, not the water. You can see this for yourself. Try making some waves in the bathtub by pushing the water with your hands. Put a rubber duck or a small ball that floats in the water and

Stormy winds can make the water lash against the shore.

watch what happens. The object just bobs up and down. It's not really pulled along by the waves.

Once a wave is started, it doesn't need the wind to keep on going. Suppose the wind stops—or say the waves were the kind made by a powerboat on a calm day—the waves still travel all the way to shore. And there on the shore you can watch and listen to their regular "splash roll," "splash roll," one after another. Maybe they are the best "rhythm" wonders on planet earth!

What Is the Ocean Floor Like?

See for yourself how the ocean floor looks. Hop aboard the magic bathyscaph (BATH uh skaf). It's an underwater boat. *Bathyscaph* comes from Greek words meaning "deep" and "bowl" or "tub." Let's go deep under the Atlantic Ocean and across the floor.

Start out at the east coast of North America. Lower your ship into the ocean and onto the part of the continent that stretches underwater. This part is called the continental shelf. It slants gently downward and is covered with sediment—bits of sand, rock, and clay.

Every continent has a continental shelf, but the shelves are not all the same width. Some are barely there, such as the shelf along the western coast of South America. Others measure up to 750 miles (1,200 kilometers) wide, like the shelf off part of the Arctic coast.

Hang on tight! You have passed the edge of the shelf and are rolling down the continental slope. Feel like an egg in a blender? The reason is that the ship is bouncing off the hills and in and out of the canyons on the slope.

BAM! You have hit bottom. Imagine falling off an average-sized mountain. That

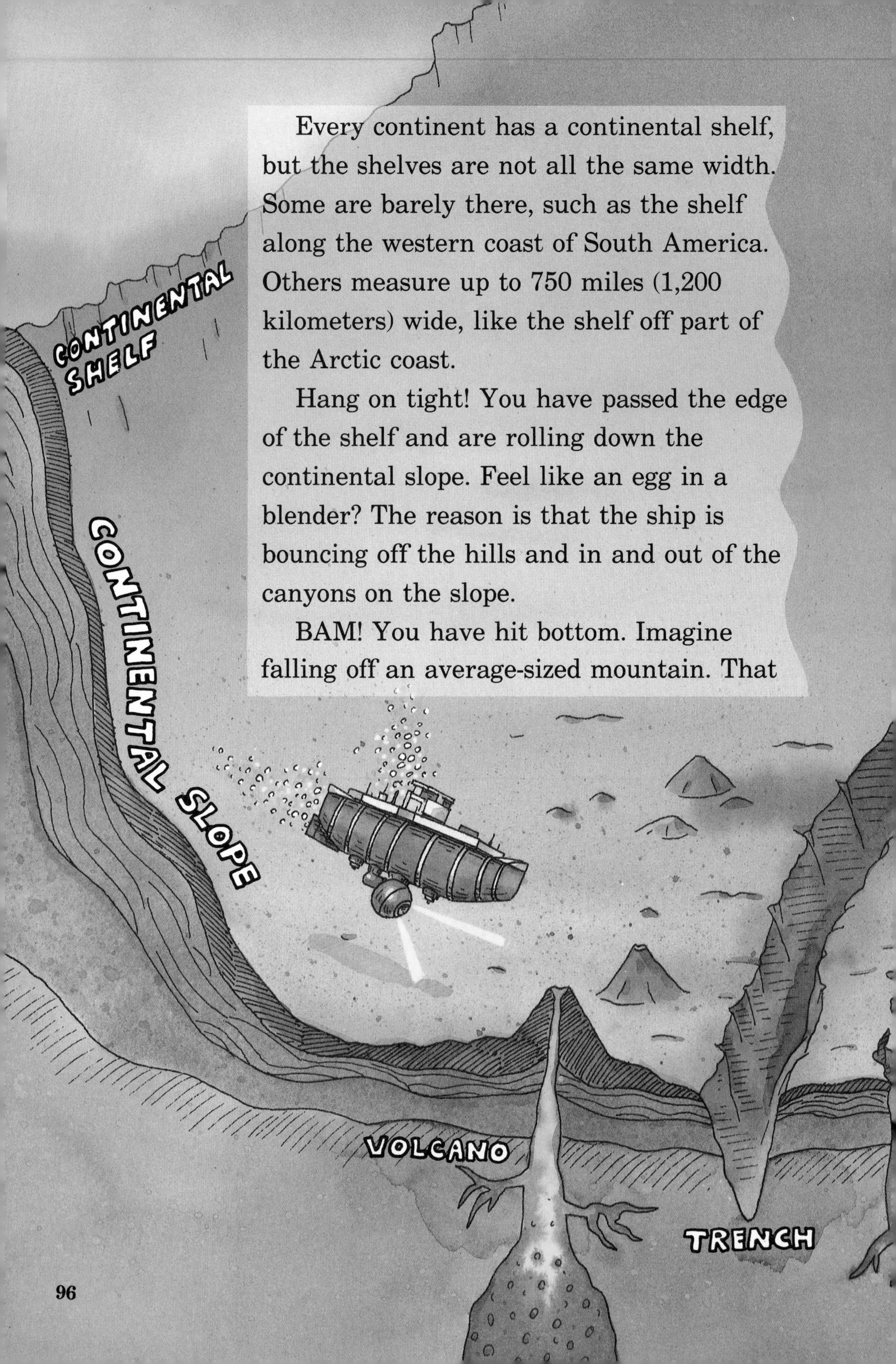

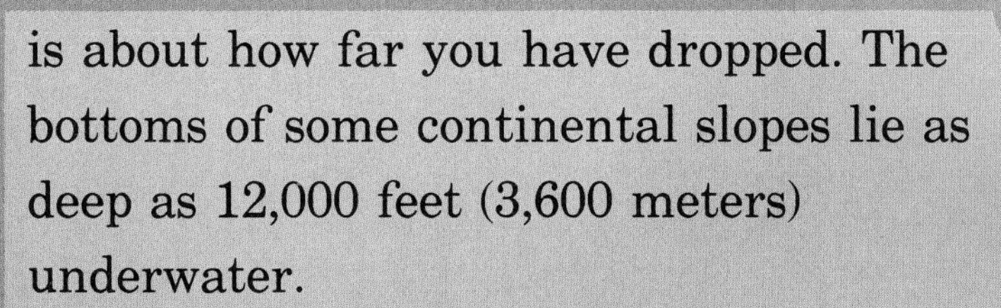

is about how far you have dropped. The bottoms of some continental slopes lie as deep as 12,000 feet (3,600 meters) underwater.

Keep the controls steady now. You may find yourself heading into powerful currents. These are moving streams of water, like rivers, within the ocean. They travel from the continental shelves to the deep ocean floor.

Next you come to mostly flat plain. It will be smooth sailing for a while. But look out for an occasional underwater volcano. Oops! Sorry. I forgot to warn you that the plain has a few canyons, too. Slow down as you come to the middle of the ocean. There you find a ridge, or chain of high, underwater volcanoes. Melted rock pours out of the volcanoes, building the ridge even higher.

Now set your controls for a super leap. Ready? Step up the power. Way to go! You have cleared the ridge. On the other side of the ridge, get ready for some more flat plains and currents. Tired? Hang on just a little longer, because here you are at the base of another continental slope. Coast up a bit. Soon you'll be high and dry again, enjoying the sun and sand of life on land.

How Can You Clean an Ocean?

Hello there. Did you ever meet a microbe? Well, that's what I am. Normally, you can't see microbes because we are so tiny. But thanks to a high-powered microscope, I am appearing to you "live" today. The ocean is my home. Lately, oil spills from ships have been messing up the ocean. Luckily, nature has ways of cleaning up some of the oil.

First, the sun goes to work. It evaporates the lighter parts of the oil. This means that the sun changes about one-third of the oil into a gas. The gas rises out of the water and spreads out into the air. The thicker, harder-to-get-rid-of parts of the oil stay in the water.

Next, some of this thick, heavy oil sticks to sand, shells, or other sediment. The weight of the oil causes the sediment to sink. In this way, some heavy oil is dropped to the bottom of the ocean, where it may be less harmful.

Then, I help take care of the rest. We microbes eat oil quickest when it is spread thinly across the water's surface. Sometimes waves whip the oil into a foam nicknamed "chocolate mousse." This foam forms thick floating sheets. As tasty as chocolate mousse looks, microbes find big globs of oil hard to swallow.

Cold also slows down our eating. Oil does not spread out in cold water as quickly as it

does in warmer water. So microbes cannot break down the oil as quickly as we can if the oil is thinly spread out.

Some spills are too big for nature alone. Then people have to pitch in. Many times, clean-up workers want to keep the oil in one place. They put booms, or floating barriers, in the water. These can help keep the oil from spreading if the water is calm. Certain booms soak up oil like paper towels soak up spills.

Sometimes clean-up workers skim oil away instead of soaking it up. Picture a cook skimming fat off the top of a soup. The cook

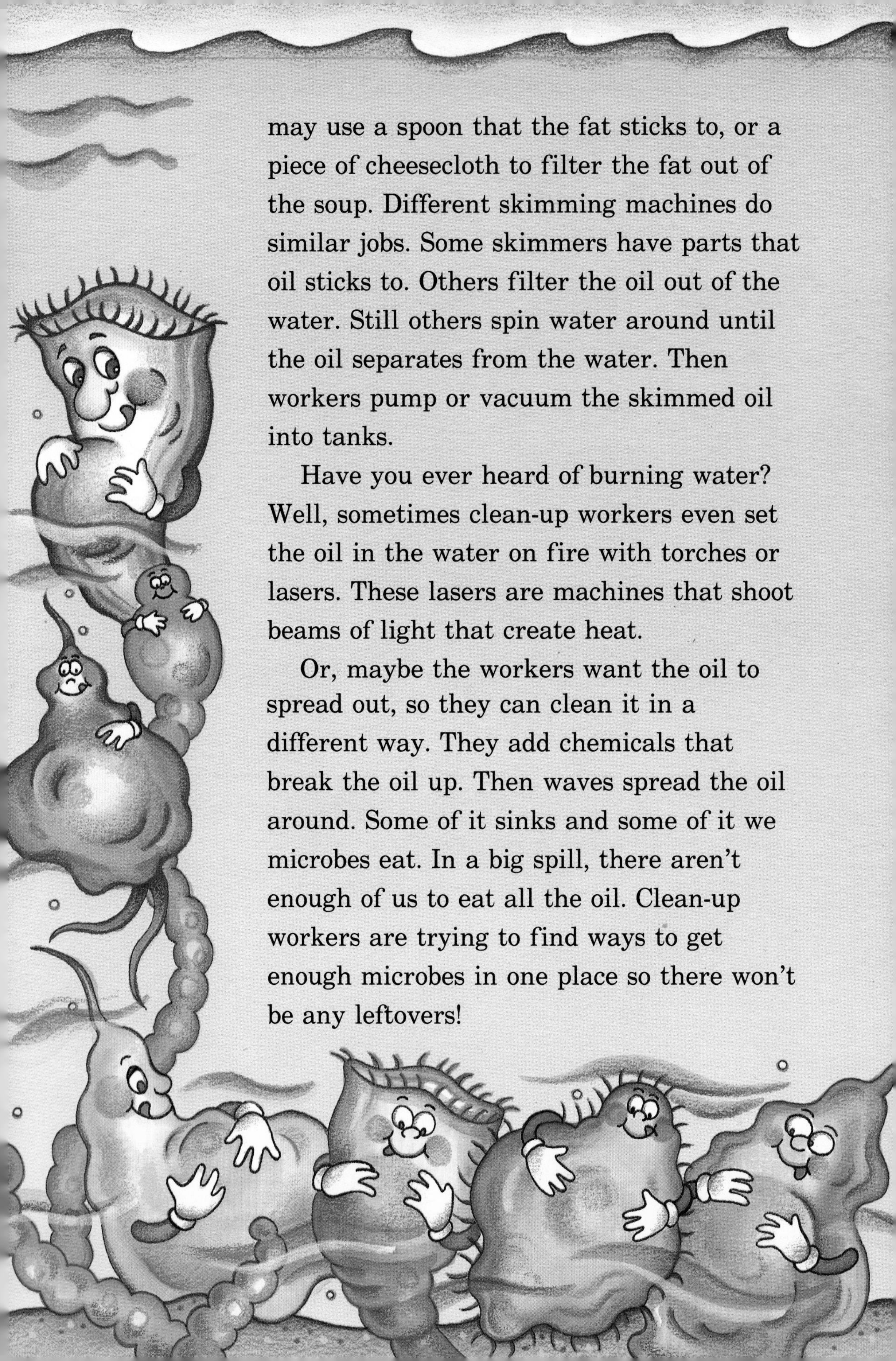

may use a spoon that the fat sticks to, or a piece of cheesecloth to filter the fat out of the soup. Different skimming machines do similar jobs. Some skimmers have parts that oil sticks to. Others filter the oil out of the water. Still others spin water around until the oil separates from the water. Then workers pump or vacuum the skimmed oil into tanks.

Have you ever heard of burning water? Well, sometimes clean-up workers even set the oil in the water on fire with torches or lasers. These lasers are machines that shoot beams of light that create heat.

Or, maybe the workers want the oil to spread out, so they can clean it in a different way. They add chemicals that break the oil up. Then waves spread the oil around. Some of it sinks and some of it we microbes eat. In a big spill, there aren't enough of us to eat all the oil. Clean-up workers are trying to find ways to get enough microbes in one place so there won't be any leftovers!

Simple Science*

What happens to oil in water?

Things you need
clear jar with tight lid
1 teaspoon cooking oil
water
dishwashing liquid

1. Fill the jar about two-thirds full with water.
2. Add the teaspoon of cooking oil and watch what happens. Does the oil mix with water, or does it stay in a blob or two at the top of the water?

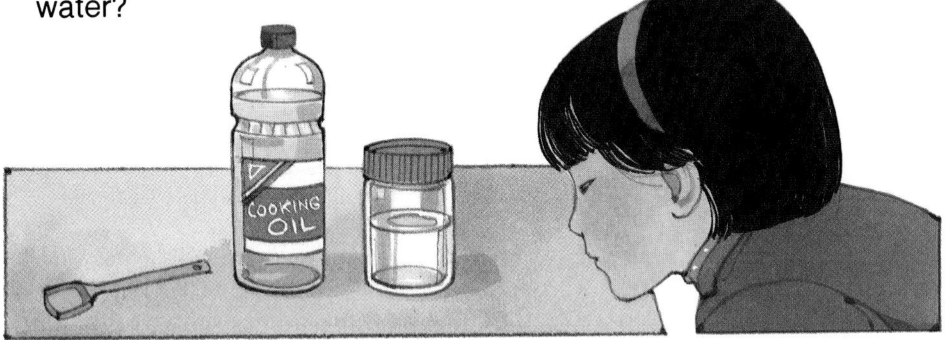

3. Now shake the jar. The oil should spread out in small bubbles, as though "waves" were tossing it around.
4. Add 2-3 drops of dishwashing liquid. Shake the jar again. Cleaning detergents break up oil into tiny droplets and spread it through the water.

*Get permission first.

Space Wonders

Questions at Night

Why
Is the sky?

What starts the thunder overhead?
Who makes the crashing noise?
Are the angels falling out of bed?
Are they breaking all their toys?

Why does the sun go down so soon?
Why do the night-clouds crawl
Hungrily up to the new-laid moon
And swallow it, shell and all?

If there's a bear among the stars,
As all the people say,
Won't he jump over those Pasture-bars
And drink up the Milky Way?

Does every star that happens to fall
Turn into a fire-fly?
Can't it ever get back to heaven at all?

And why
Is the sky?

—Louis Untermeyer

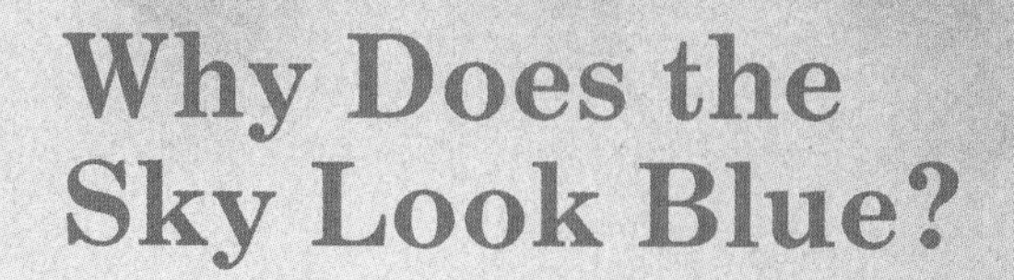

Why Does the Sky Look Blue?

It's a beautiful sunny day! When you look up, you see only blue sky. Why does the sky look blue? Why isn't it yellow or green or some other color? For the answer, let's see what happens to sunlight as it passes through the air around our earth.

Did you know that sunlight is actually made up of all the colors of the rainbow? All together, these colors make sunlight look white. When the sun's rays pass through the air, they bump into tiny particles of gas and dust in the atmosphere. These particles scatter sunlight. That is, they send it off in different directions. The atmosphere scatters more of the blue rays than the other colors in sunlight. When we look up, we see the result: the scattered blue light that we call a blue sky.

But on a sunny day, the sky doesn't simply stay blue. Around sunset, it turns to a beautiful orange and red. What makes this happen? Once again, it has to do with scattered sunlight. Late in the day, the sun is near the horizon. Its light has to pass through much more air to reach us. There are so many particles of gas and dust in the way now that almost none of the blue light can reach our eyes. By the time the sunlight does reach us, we see scattered colors that are left. These are orange and red—the colors of day's end.

You can't really "see" light scatter, but you can see the results: a blue or reddish-pink sky.

How does sunlight separate?

Things you need:
small mirror
glass of water
sunny window
light-colored ceiling or wall

1. Put the mirror in the jar of water and place the jar on a window sill in direct sunlight, with the sun hitting the mirror.

2. Look for a small patch of color to be reflected onto the ceiling or wall.

3. How many colors can you find? These are the visible colors of sunlight. The water helps to "bend" sunlight, separating it into the different colors that make up the white light. The mirror helps reflect the sunlight so you can see it projected on the wall or ceiling.

*Get permission first.

Why Do Astronauts Float?

Have you ever seen pictures of astronauts in orbit around the earth? They do not stand inside their spaceship. They float! When they are in orbit around the earth the astronauts experience something called weightlessness. What is weightlessness? Why don't we float around on the earth? The answer has to do with gravity. Gravity is the force that causes every object in the universe to pull on every other object. The

Crew members on the space shuttle *Challenger* work as they float.

more an object weighs, the stronger the pull of its gravity. Because the earth weighs so much, its gravity is strong.

You can't actually feel gravity. What you feel is the force of something pushing against you, holding you up. When you're sitting down, the chair holds you up. If you go for a walk, the earth itself holds you up. And if you're flying in an airplane, the airplane holds you up. Wherever you go, the earth's gravity pulls on you toward itself until something holds you up.

If you want to see how strong the earth's gravity is, try fighting it. Jump up in the air. For a moment, you soar upward—it looks like you're going to win! But an instant later you stop rising and fall back to earth. Gravity wins. Earth's gravity is strong enough to keep everything—people, chairs, houses—firmly on the ground. It's so strong that astronauts need a very powerful rocket to get into space.

Once they are in orbit, the astronauts and their spaceship are still pulled by earth's gravity. If so, then why do they float? They float because they are falling. They don't feel the earth's gravity because nothing is pushing against them, the way the ground holds us up. The floor of the falling spaceship does not push against the astronauts, but they do not realize they are falling. To them, the spaceship does not seem to be moving at all. With its tremendous speed, the spaceship in orbit "falls" smoothly around earth and not back down into the earth. Gravity *seems* to have vanished. Everything floats! Do you want to get from one part of the ship to another? Just push off the wall with your fingertips—not too hard, though—and off you go. Need a break from taking pictures? Just

How Does Gravity Work on the Moon?

Have you ever seen a video of astronauts walking on the moon? They bounce, as if they were walking on a trampoline. Even though they wear heavy space suits and backpacks, they can jump high in the air. Why is this so?

The moon's gravity is much less than that of the earth. Lunar, or moon, gravity is only one-sixth as strong as earth's. If you weigh sixty pounds on earth, you'd weigh only ten pounds on the moon. Imagine how high you could jump! Even the astronauts couldn't resist jumping like kangaroos every now and then. Although they worked hard, they all say walking on the moon was great fun.

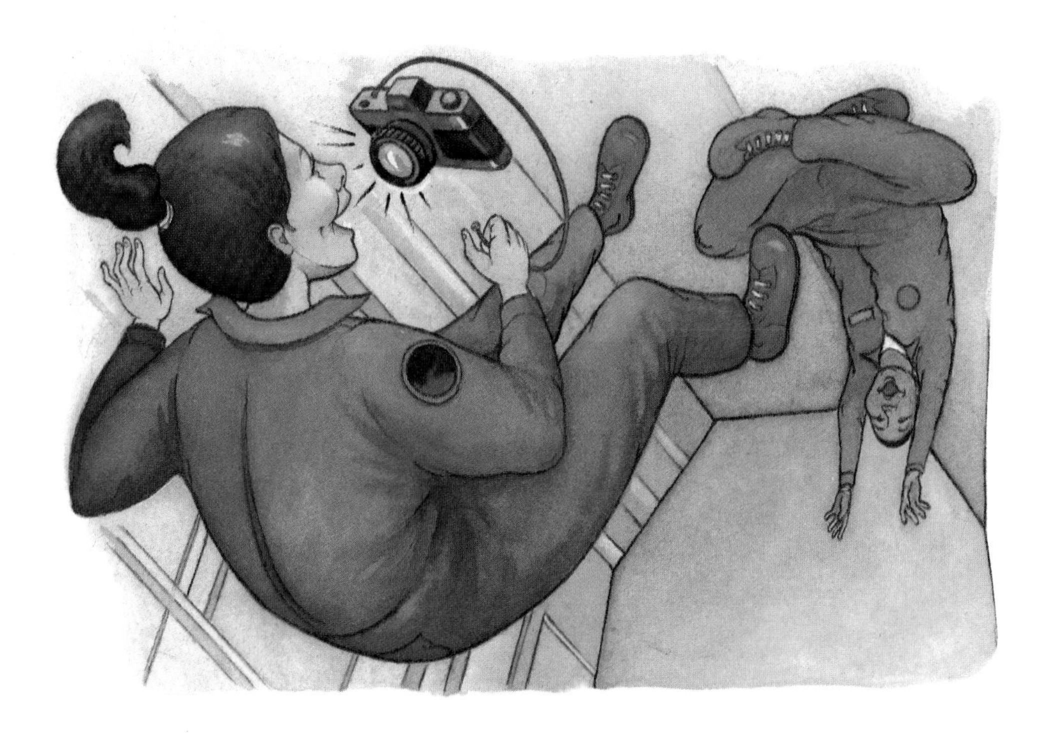

leave the camera in the air—it will stay there! On earth, gravity tells us where up and down are. When something falls, it falls down. But in space, there is no "up" or "down." The ceiling can be the floor, or the wall. You decide!

As you might imagine, being weightless for a very long time would affect your body. When the astronauts come back to earth, they are no longer used to gravity. For a time, they feel very heavy. But that feeling goes away after a few days. And even though they are glad to be back on earth, the astronauts will tell you that weightlessness is worth going back for.

Why the Sun and the Moon Live in the Sky

a folk tale from Africa

A long, long time ago, the sun and the water lived together on earth and they were great friends. They spent a lot of time together, dancing and frolicking on the beach. Very often, the sun would go to the water's house for a visit, but the water never visited the sun. The sun and his wife, the moon, lived together in a warm, cheery house. The house was painted yellow, pink, and gold, and light danced all around it. As time went by, the sun started wondering why the water never came to his house.

One day, the sun went to the water's house to talk to his friend. The water's house was very different from the sun's. It was larger, and it was painted blue, green, and violet. A breeze surrounded the house like a lullaby, and it was very peaceful.

After greeting the water, the sun asked him why he never visited his house. The sea replied, "I would very much like to visit you, but your house is not big enough. My family is very large, and if I visited you with all of my people, there wouldn't be any room for you and your wife! Now if you build a very large house, big enough to fit all of my family, I would love to come visit you in your beautiful new house," the water said. The sun thought this was a wonderful idea, and told the water he would begin planning his new house that very day.

The sun told the moon of his plans for their new house, and the two of them went to work right away. After a week, the house was finished. It was so big that it stretched as far as the eye could see. The sun said to his wife, "Surely, the water will come visit us now." And they planned a party for the water's visit, which would be the very next day.

When the water arrived at the sun's house, a band was playing a welcome song and bright banners streamed from the windows. "May I come in?" the water asked the sun and moon. "Of course, dear friend," they replied. So the water and all the members of his family began to flow into the doors. There were tiny fish that darted past the sun and moon, and huge, old whales that floated by. A parade of crabs, snails, and horseshoe crabs followed, clackety-clacking as they went. Creatures of every color, shape, and size poured into the sun's house, as the water waved them in.

Soon the water was knee-deep. It splashed gaily against the walls in time to the music. "Should we keep coming in?" the water asked the sun. "Of course!" the sun replied.

"The party's just beginning!" So more water entered the house. After a while, there was so much water trying to get through the doors that it started entering through the windows. The water danced and the seaweed waved as more and more water entered the house.

Soon, the water was high enough to cover a person's head. It almost reached the ceiling. Again, the water asked the sun if he and his family could keep coming in the house, and again, the sun said, "Of course!" So more and more water flowed in the

house, and more and more creatures flowed in the windows and doors.

Finally, there was so much water in the house that the sun and moon had to sit on the roof. "Should we keep coming in?" the water asked. The sun and moon were having too much fun to know any better, so they let more water into the house. Still more water and sea creatures streamed into the house, until finally there was no room left in the house at all. So the sun and the moon had to go up in the sky, where they have remained ever since.

What's an Eclipse?

Imagine that it's completely dark outside—in the middle of the day! That's what happens during a total eclipse of the sun. What is an eclipse of the sun?

Every once in a while, the moon passes directly in front of the sun as seen from some spot on earth. Even though the moon is much smaller than the sun, it covers it completely. How can that be? Try this experiment. Look at some large object, like a car, and close one eye. Move your thumb until you can't see the car anymore, just your thumb. Your thumb is much smaller

Going, going, gone: A total solar eclipse happens in stages.

than the car, and yet it blocks out the car. The reason is that your thumb is much closer to you than the car is to you.

The same thing happens when the moon passes in front of the sun. The moon is 400 times smaller than our giant star, but it's also about 400 times closer to us. About once every eighteen months, the moon passes in front of the sun when it is just the right distance from us to block out the sun perfectly. That's when a total eclipse can happen.

To see a total eclipse, you have to be in the right place at the right time. You have to be in the spot where the moon's shadow falls on the earth. That's right—the moon casts a shadow just like anything else, and it's only within the central part of this shadow, which is called the umbra (UHM brah), that the sun is completely covered up—a total eclipse. In the outer parts of the shadow, called the penumbra (pih NUHM brah), the sun is only partly covered. This is called a partial eclipse.

As the moon moves in its orbit, the umbra moves too, and it traces a line across the earth. For the eclipse of July 11, 1991, the umbra reaches the island of Hawaii early in the morning. Then it sweeps across the Pacific Ocean to reach Baja California, and continues on to Mexico. Next, it heads down through Central America, where it is afternoon. Finally, it reaches central Brazil just as the sun is setting.

What would you see during a total eclipse if you were in the right place? Remember, it's not safe to look directly at the sun. The safest way to look at an eclipse is to watch it indirectly. With a grown-up, punch a small round hole into a card. Hold the card in one hand and aim it so the sun shines through the hole and onto another plain white card you hold in your other hand or tape on the wall. Watch the sun's image change as it shines on the white card.

On the image, the sun looks like someone took a bite out of one edge—that's the moon, beginning to cross in front of the sun. As an hour or so passes, the bite gets bigger as the moon moves in its orbit. Now the sun looks like a crescent moon. As the crescent gets thinner, the sky gets darker. The air grows chilly. Birds and other animals sense that night may be coming soon.

Finally, there is only the barest sliver of sun left. Then it happens: The sun is completely covered! For a few minutes, the sky is very dark, almost as dark as night. And for this brief period of time, which astronomers call totality, it is okay to look at the sun. And it looks so strange! White

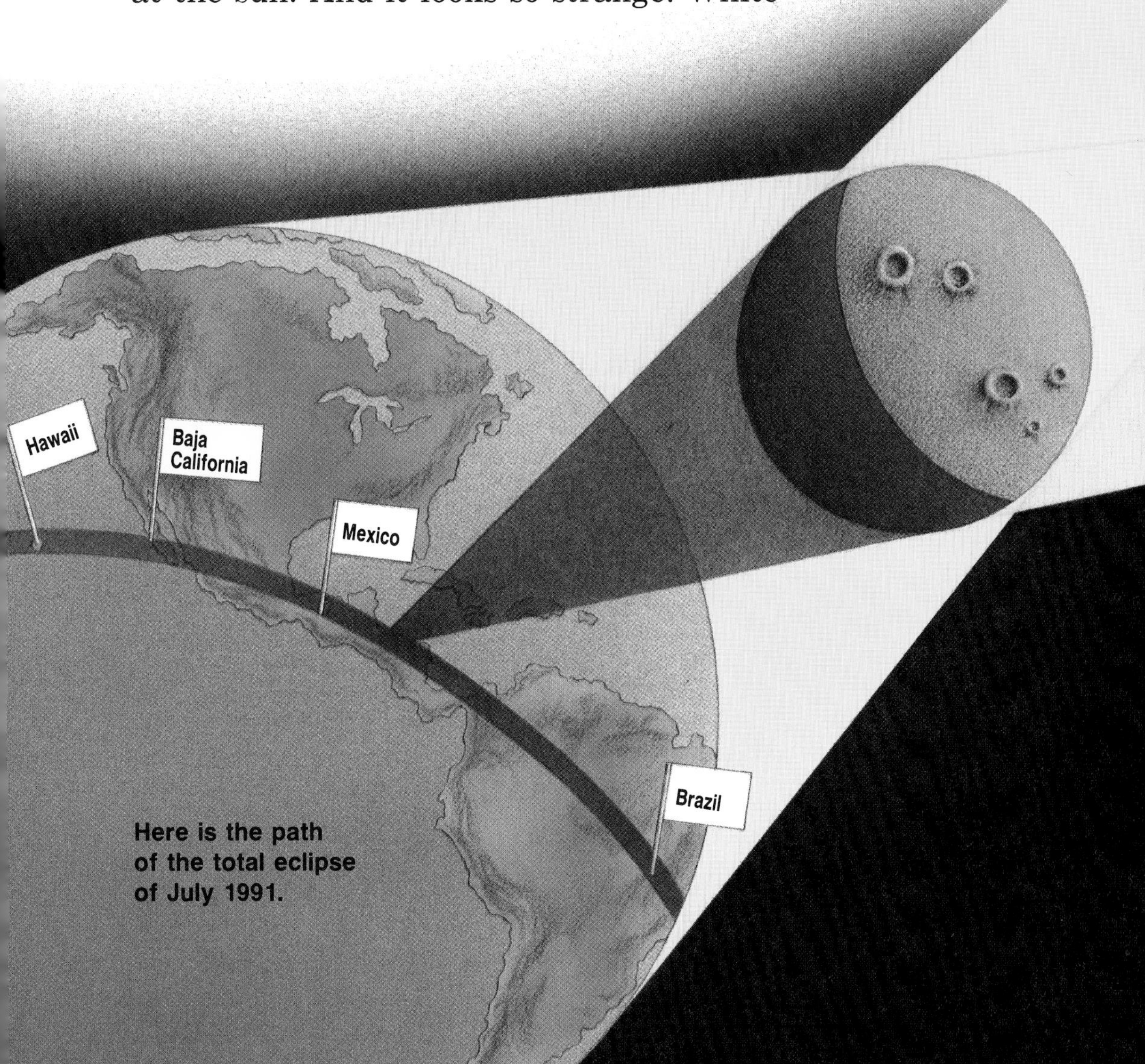

Here is the path of the total eclipse of July 1991.

A dark day—it's a solar eclipse!

wisps stretch outward from the blackened sun like the petals of a flower. This is the sun's outer atmosphere, called the corona. After totality, don't look! The sun slowly reappears, first as a thin crescent, then more and more until it is whole again. The eclipse is over—but there will be another, somewhere in the world, before too long.

Simple Science*

How can the moon block out the sun?

Things you need:
rubber ball
cup or glass
clay
flashlight
pencil

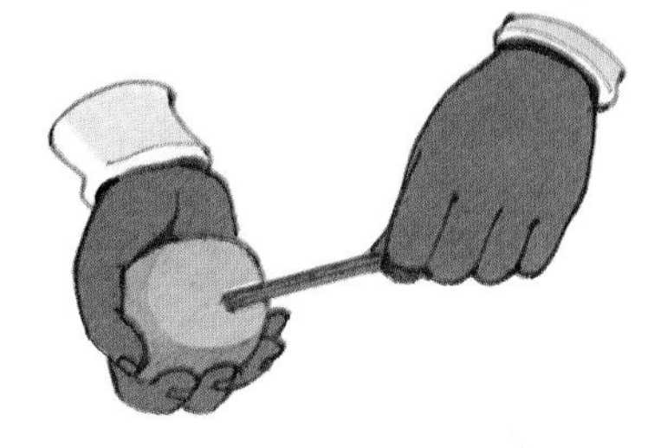

1. Place the rubber ball onto the glass or cup and put it on a table. This will be earth.

2. Roll a piece of clay into a ball that is one-fourth the size of your earth ball. Stick a pencil into the ball of clay. The clay ball will be the moon.

3. Shine the flashlight toward the earth to act as the sun.

4. Move the moon counterclockwise in orbit around earth until it is between the sun and earth.

5. Do you see the shadow on earth? The sunlight will not reach earth because the moon is blocking it, causing an eclipse.

*Get permission first.

Is Anyone Out There?

Have you ever looked up into a dark, starry sky and wondered if there was anyone out there looking back at you? Scientists wonder too. Could there be intelligent life somewhere else in the universe? No one knows the answer. In fact, no one is sure

whether life of any kind exists beyond the earth.

The other worlds of our own solar system aren't very friendly. The moon, for example, has no atmosphere and no water, and both are necessary for life as we know it. Mars, which was long thought to be the planet most like Earth, also has too little atmosphere and water. Mercury, closest planet to the sun, doesn't have enough of an atmosphere and it's unbearably hot. Daytime temperatures reach about 800 °F (427 °C). Venus, under its thick clouds, is even hotter—about 900 °F (482 °C). Think of a 90-degree day—ten times worse!

What of the giant planets—Jupiter, Saturn, Uranus, and Neptune? They have thick, cloudy atmospheres that we couldn't survive in. They are also very cold. Jupiter's cloud tops are about 250 °F below zero (−157 °C). Does that sound cold? Remember, water turns to ice at 32 °F *above* zero (0 °C). For now, it doesn't seem likely that there is life in our solar system beyond the earth!

Many scientists believe there could be life beyond our little neighborhood in space, even perhaps other intelligent beings. Why do they say this? The main reason is because the universe is so very big.

Think of that dark, starry sky. There are so many stars in the universe that people often compare them to the grains of sand on a beach. Astronomers estimate that there are hundreds of billions of stars in our Milky Way galaxy. We know of millions of galaxies in the universe, each with many billions of stars. That's a lot of stars!

Astronomers reason that with so many stars, there might be other planets with the right conditions for life. What if there is intelligent life out there? Even a few civilizations? Now that would be an exciting discovery! For the first time we would know there is "someone" out there.

I Wonder What This Is.

Clue: Take a good look. You wouldn't want to live here, but it's a fascinating place to look at.

Find the answer on page 243.

Weather Wonders

?

?

Why Do Clouds Look Different?

Look at the sky. Are the clouds bright and fluffy, like woolly sheep? Are they dark and gloomy? Or are they thin and wispy, like delicate white feathers? What makes clouds? Why do they look different?

Clouds are made from droplets of water, or ice crystals, floating in the air. There is always some water in the air. You can't see it because it is in the form of a gas called water vapor. In the summer, when it's warm, you can sense the water in the air. We say that it's humid.

On cold days, the air often seems dry. That's because cold air can't hold as much water vapor as warm air. When it's very cold, you can make a cloud simply by breathing out, *exhaling*. The breath you exhale is warmer and moister than the

surrounding air. When you exhale on a cold day, the air quickly cools your breath. As your breath cools, it cannot hold as much moisture. This causes the water vapor in it to change from gas to liquid, to condense. A cloud is formed when water vapor condenses into tiny water droplets.

The clouds in the sky are made when water vapor condenses, too. Air that is close to the ground is warmed by the land. This warm air can hold a lot of moisture. However, higher up in the sky, the air is cooler. Cooler air cannot hold as much water vapor as warm air. When warm air rises it expands and cools. As it expands and cools,

Stratus Clouds:
***Stratus* means "layer."**

much of the water vapor condenses on microscopic dust particles. Millions of tiny water droplets form. These droplets make clouds.

Why don't all clouds look the same? To answer that question, we need to look at the air. Is it moving? How fast is it moving? How warm is it? How cold is it?

Sometimes the air is fairly still. A sheet of warm air may come rolling in over a sheet of colder air. The two sheets meet and form a thick layer of clouds. Clouds formed this way are called *stratus* clouds.

Sometimes the air is stirred up, and currents of warm air rise high into the sky.

High up, the air is cooler. When the warm, moist air currents cool and expand, their moisture condenses to form puffy, cottonlike clouds. These are *cumulus* (KYOO myuh luhs) clouds.

Even higher up in the sky, the air is so cold that water vapor freezes into tiny ice crystals. Wispy *cirrus* (SIHR uhs) clouds are made of ice crystals.

Keep your eyes on the clouds to find out about more weather wonders! Why does it rain and snow? What makes tornadoes, hurricanes, and rainbows? Why is there thunder and lightning? Why is it warm in some places and cold in others? Read on!

Clouds

White sheep, white sheep,
On a blue hill,
When the wind stops
You all stand still.

When the wind blows
You walk away slow.
White sheep, white sheep,
Where do you go?

—Christina Rossetti

Why Is It Raining? Snowing? Hailing?

Clouds are made of water droplets. But what causes these droplets to rain, snow, or hail down on us? The water droplets that make up clouds are extremely tiny—so tiny that even the gentlest air currents will keep them floating in the sky. What causes these droplets to fall from a cloud?

Much rain begins inside a cloud as bits of ice, not drops of water. The upper parts of a very tall cumulonimbus, or thundercloud, are cold enough for water vapor to freeze and form tiny ice crystals. Like seeds, these crystals grow in the cloud. As more water vapor condenses on the seeds, they grow bigger. When the crystals grow, little pellets of ice are formed. When the pellets become too heavy for air currents to hold up, they fall. As they fall down through the tall cloud, the pellets pass through warmer air. The warm air melts them and they turn into tiny raindrops. As they fall, the tiny

raindrops bump into each other and form bigger drops. The average raindrop has about a million times as much water as a tiny water droplet in a cloud.

Can it rain if a cloud is too warm for ice crystals to form? Only if the cloud is over the ocean. The droplets that form clouds always condense on microscopic particles in the air. Seed crystals must be formed in clouds before it rains. When it is warm, ice crystals can't form, but clouds that are over or very near the ocean make a different kind of seed. This time, the seeds for the raindrops are tiny crystals of salt from the ocean. Water droplets soon condense around the salt crystals. The water droplets bump into each other and form bigger drops.

Before long the drops are big enough and heavy enough to fall as rain.

What happens when the air both high in the sky and close to the ground is very cold? The tiny ice crystals that form inside clouds do not melt and turn to rain. Instead, they become crystals of ice. As they fall through the cloud, they gather more ice crystals and grow bigger. By the time they reach the bottom of the cloud, they have beautiful, intricate shapes. Can you guess what these are? Snowflakes!

Why is the grass wet (when it didn't rain)?

Early on a bright, clear autumn morning, you see the grass is sparkling in the sun. It's wet with tiny droplets of water. Droplets cling to a spider web like a jeweled necklace. Yet, it did not rain in the night. What happened?

Warm, moist air settled in over the ground at day's end. The air was still throughout the night. As the ground cooled, some of the moisture in the air condensed on the grass, the spider web, and all around. These droplets of water are called dew. As the sun rises, the heat dries up, *evaporates*, the dew. This evening, the cycle may begin again. By morning the grass could be shimmering with dew.

It may take more than a million tiny ice crystals to make one snowflake. Have you ever seen a snowflake up close? Some are needle-shaped. Others look more like triangles. Some look like six-pointed stars made out of lace. Look for snowflakes in these shapes and others.

Another kind of falling ice is known as hail. Hail is not delicate like snow. Like snow, it is made from ice crystals.

Sometimes, in tall cumulonimbus clouds, there are powerful air currents that keep raindrops from falling. The wind carries the drops upward to the colder parts of the cloud. There, the drops freeze into beads of ice. Each bead of ice is so heavy that it falls back down to the lower part of the cloud. Water collects around it, and if another gust of wind carries it upward again, the extra water freezes into a new layer of ice. This happens many

times. The ice bead grows bigger and bigger, until it falls to earth. These falling balls of ice are called hailstones. Because it is made in layers, the inside of a hailstone is like an onion. A hailstone can be the size of a marble, a golf ball, even a baseball! So, keep on the lookout. The clouds may be making some fresh rain, snow, or hail. With all the water in the air and the clouds, sometimes it's hard to stay dry!

Simple Science*

How is rain made?

> **Things you need:**
> a small metal cup
> steamy water
> a rubber glove or an oven mitt

1. Set the cup in the freezer for at least 15 minutes.

2. When the cup or spoon has been getting ice cold for at least 15 minutes, turn on the hot water in the kitchen sink. Leave it on until steam begins to form.
3. Put on your rubber glove or oven mitt. When you can see wisps of steam from the hot water, take the cup out of the freezer.
4. Quickly bring the cup to the steam. Hold it in the steam, away from the water. Be careful not to let any hot water splash on you or the cup.
5. Hold the cup in the steam for about a minute. What happens? Drops of water should form on the side or bottom of the cup. The freezing cold metal cools the hot steam and water droplets, or dew forms. Some drops may even fall as "rain."

*Get permission first.

Thunder and Lightning

Flaaaaaash! You see a brilliant bolt of lightning. An instant later, you hear the boom of thunder. Why did that happen?

Have you ever felt static electricity? It happens when electricity is released. You can pick up an electric charge by walking across a carpeted floor in leather-soled shoes. As your shoes rub against the carpet fibers, they pick up an electric charge. If you touch a doorknob, there is a small spark—an electric discharge.

Something similar happens inside a rain cloud. Lightning is electricity that comes

from rain clouds. The drops of water and ice in the cloud become electrically charged. After a while, the charge becomes very strong. The drops must get rid of their electric charge. Suddenly there is a spark, or electric discharge, that travels through the air. It may travel within the cloud. Or it may go from one cloud to another cloud. It might even go from the cloud down to the ground. An electric discharge from a cloud is called lightning.

A bolt of lightning contains an incredible amount of energy. It may discharge as much as 100 million volts of electricity. As it travels through the atmosphere, the bolt of

lightning very quickly makes the air around it very hot. This hot air expands outward from the lightning bolt and slams into cooler air, like a stick beating a drum. When the hot air expands we hear a BOOM! That's thunder.

When you are close to a bolt of lightning, the boom of thunder follows the flash of lightning almost instantly. When you are farther away from the lightning you have to wait a moment after the flash to hear the crack. That's because the light waves from the lightning travel much faster than the sound waves from the thunder.

There's a simple way to find out how far away a lightning bolt is. When you see a flash, count the seconds until you hear the boom of thunder. Divide the number of seconds by five. Your answer tells how many miles you are from the storm. Divide by three for the answer in kilometers.

If you're ever caught outside during a thunderstorm, be careful. If lightning strikes the ground, it usually strikes the highest place or the tallest thing in the area. During a lightning storm, don't stand under a tree, or a metal tower. Also, stay away from the water. A hardtop car is a safe place to be. The metal frame will carry the charge around you even if lightning hits the car. Even so, do not touch any metal parts of the car's frame. It's helpful to know what to do even though many bolts do not strike at all. Of course, the best thing to do in a thunderstorm is to watch the wonder of it from your window!

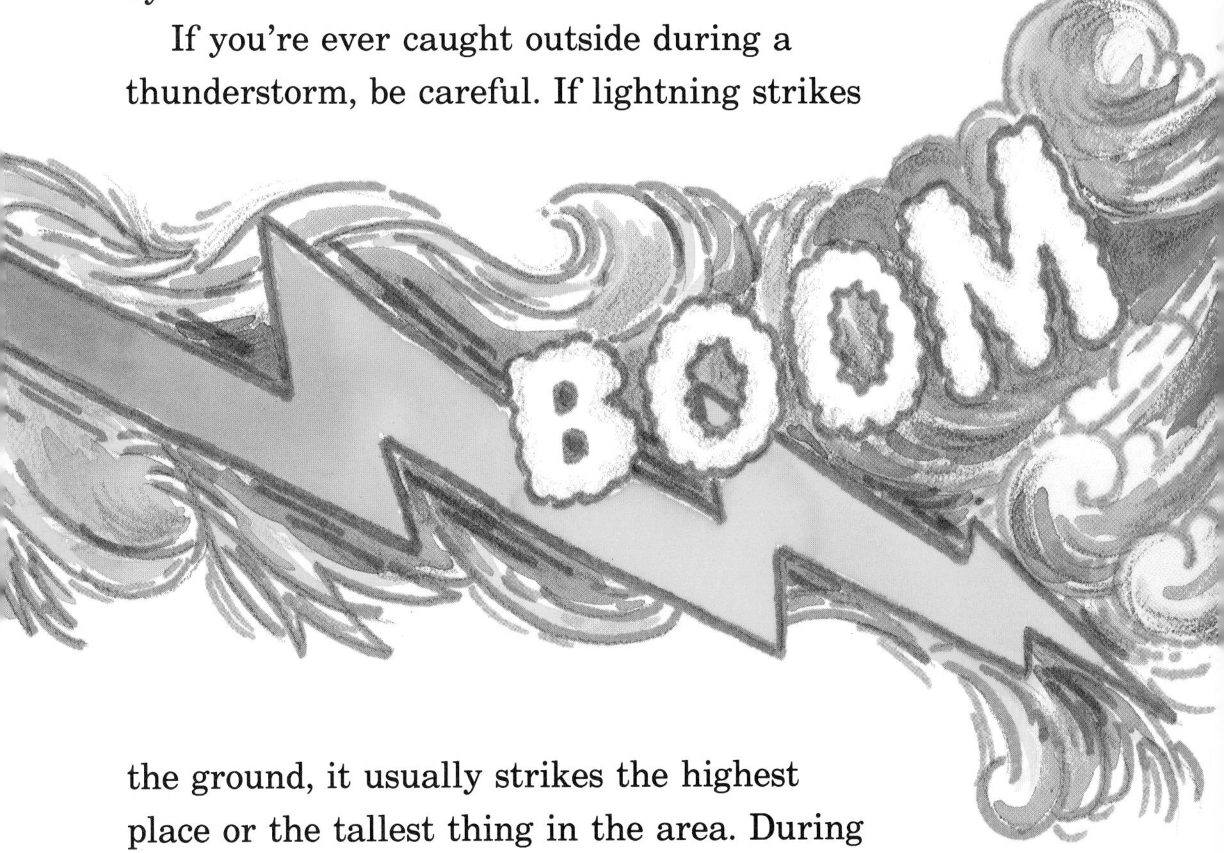

Why There Are Four Seasons in the Year

a tale told by the Chippewayan Indians, retold by Natalia Belting

In the days of the grandfathers there was no winter. There was no spring. There was no fall. It was summer all the time. Each day the sun rose and crossed the sky and there was not even a cloud to cover it to make shade for the earth.

The grass was dry and brown. The berries shriveled on the bushes. The streams and the rivers dried up. Dust hung heavily in the air.

"There is nothing to eat," Rabbit said. "Nothing to eat except dry grass."

"There is nothing to drink," Deer said, "not even a bit of dew in the morning."

"There is not even air to breathe," Bear said, "only dust," and he sneezed.

"It is too hot," Polar Bear said. "There is not even a small piece of ice to sit on."

"It is so hot," Mountain Lion said, "that the rocks blister my feet."

"It is too hot even to fly," the birds said.

"It is too hot," the animals agreed. "It is too hot. We must do something about it."

So they called a council. They set out a message on a long strip of bark. "Come to a council," it said.

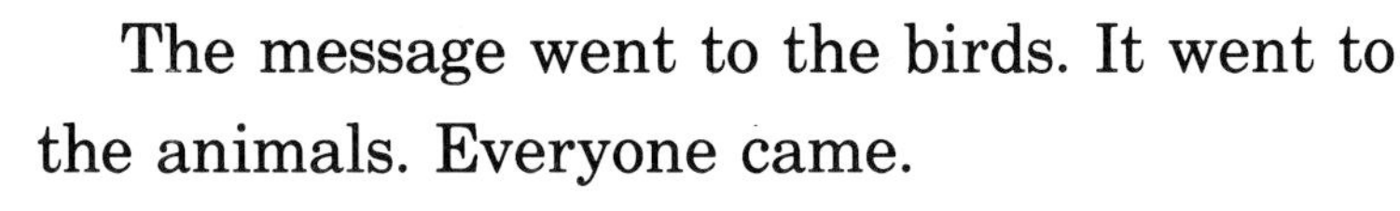

The message went to the birds. It went to the animals. Everyone came.

The council fire was built. The animals sat down on one side. The birds sat down on one side. The council began.

Rabbit spoke. "It is too hot," he said.

Owl spoke. "It is too hot," he said.

Polar Bear spoke. "We must go to the Skyland and see the old woman who lives there."

The animals agreed. The birds agreed. Owl put out the council fire.

"How do we get to the Skyland?" Rabbit asked.

"There is the road," Fox said. All the animals followed Fox to the edge of the sea. They saw the Shining Road where it touched the water. They saw the Shining Road curve up into the sky.

Fox led the way. The birds and animals followed. They traveled over the Shining Road for many moons. They left the earth behind. Now there were only the stars and the moon and the sun. There was not even dry grass. There were not even berries shriveled on the bushes. There was not any dust.

There was only the hot sun in the daytime. There was only the cold starlight at night, and the cold moonlight. It was too hot in the daytime. It was too cold in the nighttime.

Finally the animals came out upon a prairie. It stretched away to the north and to the south and to the east and to the west. Wherever they looked there was the lodge of the prairie. In the middle of it was the lodge of the old woman, the Sky Woman.

"Bear shall speak for us," the animals decided.

"Owl shall speak for us," the birds decided.

They made a circle before the door of the lodge. They sat down. Owl called to Sky Woman.

Sky Woman came out. Sky Woman was older than the earth. She was older than the sky.

Bear spoke. "It is too hot on earth," he said. "There is only brown grass. There is no water in the streams. There is only dust in the air."

Owl spoke. "We cannot live on earth any longer," he said. "There is nothing to eat. There is nothing to drink. And the sun is too hot for us."

Sky Woman took pity on the birds and the animals. Sky Woman went into the lodge. She came out again. "Take these," she

said. She gave a bag to Bear. She gave a bag to Owl. She gave a bag to Rabbit. "Take these back to the earth. When you are in your own village, open them."

The animals and the birds went back across the prairie. They went down the Shining Road. They traveled many moons and came to their village.

Bear opened his bag. The winds came out of it. The North Wind and the South Wind, the East Wind and the West Wind. They blew through the dried grass and it crackled. They blew through the bushes and the berries fell. They blew through the trees and the leaves fell to the ground.

Owl opened his bag. Rain and fog came out of it. First the fog settled down around them, and hid their lodges from them. Then the rain melted the fog, and the birds went into their lodges to keep dry. (All except Rabbit.)

Rabbit opened his bag. Snow came out of it. Heavy snow filled the air. Thick snow covered the ground.

From that day there have been the seasons. There is winter and spring and fall.

There is summer, when the sun is hot and the grass is dry and the berries shrivel and the dust hangs in the air, but always the wind and the rain and the fog come, and snow, and there is an end to summer.

This story is found in The Earth Is on a Fish's Back: Tales of Beginnings, *by Natalia Belting. Author Belting's other books include* The Sun Is a Golden Earring *and* Elves and Ellefolk: Tales of the Little People.

Why Is It Hotter or Colder in Some Places?

Why do temperatures change? Let's look to, *not at*, the sun for the answer. The sun's rays shine down on us every day. So, why are some days, places, or seasons warmer than others?

When the sun is high overhead, its rays shine almost straight down on us. We can

When the sun is low in the sky, its rays hit the earth at an angle. When that happens, we don't feel the sun's warmth.

But, if the sun is high in the sky, the rays shine their warmth directly on us.

feel the warmth. When the sun is low in the sky, it does not get as warm. This is because the sun's rays strike the earth at an angle. Think about how hot it can be at noon in the middle of the summer. The sun is directly overhead. In the winter, the sun never climbs that high in the sky.

The coolest part of the day is just before sunrise. The ground cools throughout the night. It takes a while for the sun's energy to warm the air and the ground. It takes longer for the ground to warm up than the air. Therefore, the hottest part of the day is not noon. It is around 2:00 in the afternoon. By that time, the sun has had a chance to warm both the air and the ground.

Temperatures not only are different throughout a day, but in different places. If you lived near the equator, in a place where there were no mountains, you'd feel heat in the air and on the ground most of the year. That's quite different from the polar regions, where there is always ice and snow.

What makes summer warmer than winter? Remember the tilt of the earth as it revolves around the sun changes the amount of heat we get. (You can read more about this on pages 57-61.) Doesn't it make sense that the hottest part of the earth is the part

The brown part of the earth is warm desert.
The white part is the frozen polar ice cap.

that is tilted toward the sun? The Northern Hemisphere reaches the point of its greatest tilt toward the sun in June. It is summer there from June to September. In contrast, the Southern Hemisphere is more in line with the sun in December. It is summer there from December to March. Where would you enjoy being in January? A sunny, summery place or a cold, wintry place? The earth has different temperatures in different places, at different times of the year. Where on earth would you like to live?

Rainbows

If I could climb
  the mountains
And rest on clouds
  that float
I'd swim across
  the clear blue air
To reach my rainbow boat

My rainbow boat
  is oh so big
And I could be
  so tall
As I sit
  in my captain's chair
The master of it all

But I am just a little boy
  who's standing on the ground
And others steer
  the rainbow past
While I just hang around

I sit on the ground
  and see
The rainbows steering
  right past me
I sit on the ground
And wonder *why*

—Nikki Giovanni

The True Story of Rainbows

Have you heard the story of the pot of gold at the end of the rainbow? Awed by the beauty of rainbows, people long ago made up stories about them. Today we know the true story of rainbows.

Rainbows come out when the sun shines while the air is full of raindrops. The recipe for a rainbow is simple. You need air that is full of raindrops mixed with sunshine, and *ta DAH!* A rainbow may appear.

How is the white light of the sun broken up into a rainbow of colors? Why do we see red, orange, yellow, green, blue, and violet when sun shines through a raindrop? Raindrops can act like prisms. When sunlight goes into the raindrop it is white, but it comes out split into the colors of the rainbow. When the sun shines on many raindrops in the air, the colors form a curved band—a rainbow.

A rainbow looks like an arch, but it really isn't. Did you know that we can only see half of a rainbow? If we could look down on a rainbow from an airplane, we would see that it forms a complete circle. Since we usually see them from the ground, we only see half of the circle. The half-circle forms an arch. The arch looks like a bridge. No wonder people wanted to cross it to see what was on the other side.

Almost a full rainbow. Can you picture what the rest looks like?

Hurricanes and Tornadoes: Be Alert!

All along the coastline, people are covering their windows and gathering supplies. Some people are packing up to leave their homes until the coming storm passes. Why do you think they are doing this? A hurricane is coming!

A hurricane is a storm that begins in the middle of the ocean. It forms when winds blowing in opposite directions meet. They swirl around each other. The swirling winds trap the warm, moist ocean air.

As the winds swirl, the water vapor in the trapped air condenses. Rain clouds form and a storm is born. This is not an ordinary rainstorm. How does a hurricane differ from other storms?

When water vapor condenses into water droplets, heat is released. This heat makes the winds swirl faster. It also pulls more warm air up from the ocean. This causes the storm to grow stronger. So, more rain clouds are formed and more winds swirl around it. The storm grows to be hundreds of miles wide. When the winds inside it move at 74 miles (118 kilometers) per hour or faster, the storm is called a hurricane.

Covering up windows before the hurricane comes helps keep glass from flying.

The center of the hurricane is called the eye. Here it is calm. The eye of a hurricane is about 20 miles (32 kilometers) across. Inside the eye, there is little wind. Just outside the eye, the winds can reach 150 miles (240 kilometers) per hour.

If a hurricane didn't move, it would get larger and more powerful. But hurricanes don't stay in one place. Sometimes hurricanes move toward land. They crash into cities and towns along the coastline. When a hurricane strikes land, it destroys much of what it hits. However, once a hurricane is over land, it weakens. With its warm air supply lessened, the hurricane breaks into smaller storms and dies.

Not all hurricanes touch land, but they do eventually die. These hurricanes die because they move north, where the water is colder. Like hurricanes on land, without warm water, they can no longer fuel themselves. A hurricane generally lasts one to two weeks.

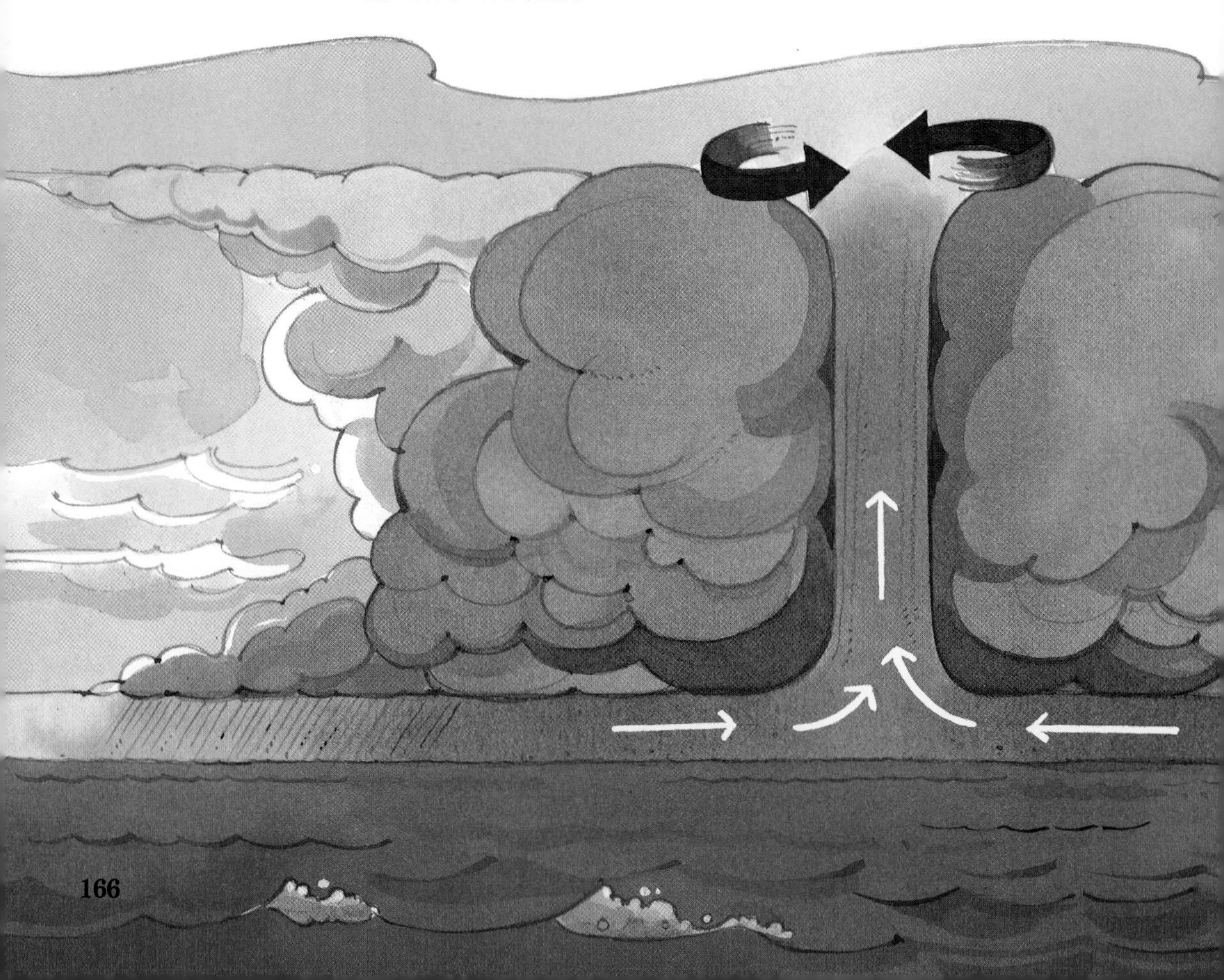

A tornado does not last as long as a hurricane, but in the half an hour that it touches down, it can cause more damage. Tornadoes are long, funnel-shaped clouds that under certain conditions can form near a line of rain clouds.

Tornadoes are not very large, only a few hundred feet (kilometers) across. It is believed that the winds inside the funnel swirl at more than 200 miles (320 kilometers) per hour. We don't know exactly how fast tornado winds move. We can't measure the winds, but we can watch the whole funnel move.

Eye of the hurricane

Hopefully this tornado is moving away from the farm.

Tornadoes have been known to throw trucks in the air and uproot trees. They cause a lot of damage because they can lift up and touch down several times. Fortunately, tornadoes do not last long. Even the strongest only last about half an hour.

The average speed of a tornado is only about 25 miles (40 kilometers) per hour. As hurricanes can only form over water, tornadoes can only form over land. Although these storms may be scary, they are as natural and normal on earth as rainbows.

Simple Science*

How do winds change?

1. Cut off the sleeve of an old shirt to make a wind sock.

Things you need:
old shirtsleeve
thin, flexible wire
stapler
string
needle and thread
scissors

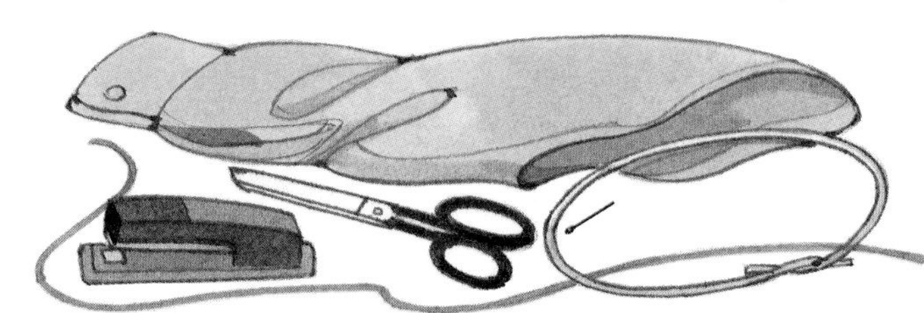

2. Measure the wire to fit the shoulder of the sleeve. Bend the wire into a circle the size of the sleeve opening.

3. Staple the edge of the sleeve over the wire. Have a grown-up help you sew the cloth to the wire. Slip the string between the wire and sleeve before you finish sewing.

4. Tie the wind sock to a tree branch.

5. Watch what happens over several days. Sometimes the sock will hardly move. Other times the wind will blow right through it. The force of the wind changes and so does the direction. How does your wind sock react to the wind?

*Get permission first.

Frost on the Window

Imagine that it's a cold winter morning. Look out the window, and what do you see? The glass is decorated with beautiful, feathery patterns. The "feathers" that you see are ice crystals called frost. Did Jack Frost come in the middle of the night and decorate your windows? If not, how did the frost get there?

Remember that there is water vapor in the air, even when it is cold. Well, that water vapor came into contact with your window. In the night, the winter air made the glass very cold. When the water vapor condensed, it froze and turned into ice. Also, there are scratches and particles of dust and dirt on your windows. These act like seeds for ice crystals to grow on. At first, the crystals are too small for you to see. But, as more moisture touched the glass, the crystals grew. As they grew, delicate patterns took shape on your window.

Frost does not stay on your windows all day. As the sun warms the glass, the ice melts. The water evaporates and with it goes the pretty picture.

I Wonder What This Is.

Clue: Soft as a feather, but if you reached out to stroke it, it would disappear!

Find the answer on page 243.

Wondrous Creatures

?

?

To the Skeleton of a Dinosaur in the Museum

Hey there, Brontosaurus!
You were here so long before us
Your deeds can never bore us.
How *were* the good old days?

Did you really like to graze?
Did you often munch
With a prehistoric crunch
On a giant tree—or two—or three
For lunch?

As you went yon and hither
Were you ever in a dither
When your head and distant tail
Went different ways?

Did you shake the earth like thunder
With your roars and groans?
I wonder. . . . Say it's hard
To have a conversation
With your bones.

—Lilian Moore

Any New News About Dinosaurs?

Dinosaurs, those amazing creatures of long ago, are still as fascinating as ever. And scientists are learning more about them all the time. What's new about dinosaurs?

One important fossil (FAHS uhl) discovery took place in China in 1987. If you're a dinosaur lover, you know that fossils are the remains of plants or animals that lived long ago. Maybe the fossil is the print of the living thing found in rock, or in ice or mud. The new discovery was wonderful: the skeleton of a new type of prehistoric animal. This was no ordinary dinosaur. When it lived, it had feathers. What was it?

In some ways, the new skeleton was like a bird's. But in other ways, the bones were like a dinosaur's. Scientists have long believed that birds are descended from dinosaurs, and this fossil added more proof. Back in 1861, scientists discovered the fossil of a winged animal about the size of a crow. They named it *Archaeopteryx* (ahr kee AHP tuhr ihks), which means "ancient wing." Although it had wings and feathers, it also had a skeleton like those of its wingless dinosaur cousins.

What is the difference between the sparrow (above) and the skeleton (below)? About 135 million years! The skeleton of the 1987 birdlike fossil is an artist's drawing.

This new fossil, however, is different. Researchers who have studied it say it is much more like the birds we see today than Archaeopteryx was. In fact, the age of the fossil is about 135 million years. This puts it halfway between Archaeopteryx, which lived ten million years earlier, and the previously discovered modern birds that lived about ten million years later.

The new fossil is only the size of a sparrow, and some of its bones were so small and delicate that scientists used a microscope to study their fossil imprint.

Speaking of birds, some scientists believe dinosaurs may have been more birdlike than they first thought. For a long time, it was thought that dinosaurs were cold-blooded, like today's reptiles. Cold-blooded animals need the sun to warm them. When they are warm, they can move quickly. When they are cold, they are slow and sluggish.

In the last several years, however, many scientists have come to agree that some dinosaurs were probably warm-blooded, like birds and mammals. If they were, then dinosaurs may have moved a lot faster than anyone ever thought. Scientists have found footprints, preserved in mud that hardened into rock, made by a dinosaur that ran for

A print of the past: This is the birdlike fossil that scientists found in China in 1987.

a long time without stopping. Today's reptiles, being cold-blooded, don't have enough energy to do that.

Dinosaurs lived such a long time ago that sometimes it's hard to believe they really existed. But they really did, and we get to learn more about them all the time.

Simple Science*

How are fossils made?

Things you need:
small foil pie plate
modeling clay or "play dough" clay
fossil form (leaf, twig, or shell, for example)
1 cup plaster of Paris (from a craft or hardware store)
1/2 cup water
stirring stick
can for mixing

1. Spread a layer of clay in the pie plate, about 1/2 inch (1.25 cm) thick.

2. Press your "fossil form" into the clay. Make sure you get a good print in the clay, and take the form out.

3. Mix the plaster of Paris and water in the mixing can. Stir it with the stick until it looks like thick cream.

4. Pour the mixture into a layer about one inch (2.5 cm) thick over the clay. Wait about 3 hours for the plaster to harden.

5. When the plaster is hard, pop it out of the pie plate. Peel the clay off to find your instant "fossil." Many real fossils formed in mud or sand. Over thousands of years, more layers of mud or sand pressed down on the lower layers and hardened them into rock.

*Get permission first.

When All the World's Asleep

Where do insects go at night,
When all the world's asleep?
Where do bugs and butterflies
And caterpillars creep?
Turtles sleep inside their shells;
The robin has her nest.
Rabbits and the sly old fox
Have holes where they can rest.
Bears can crawl inside a cave;
The lion has its den.
Cows can sleep inside the barn,
And pigs can use their pen.
But where do bugs and butterflies
And caterpillars creep,
When everything is dark outside
And all the world's asleep?

—Anita E. Posey

Little Lanterns: How Do Fireflies Light Up?

Have you ever seen fireflies glowing on a summer night? A firefly is a kind of insect that makes its own light. You can see them flash on and off like tiny light bulbs. How do they do it?

Inside the firefly's body, on its underside, is a special organ that has a substance called *luciferin* (loo sih FEH rihn). The word *luciferin* comes from Latin words that mean *light bearer*. When luciferin, with the help of other chemicals, mixes with oxygen that the firefly breathes, it gives off a weak,

greenish-yellow light. The skin around the firefly's tail lets the light shine through. Even though the firefly's light is faint—much dimmer than a candle flame—our eyes are very sensitive to its color. So the firefly looks bright to us.

Both male and female fireflies light up. Since many females don't fly, they flash from the grass or low-lying branches. The males fly by, flashing their signals from the air. Why do fireflies light up? Scientists believe they flash in order to attract a mate. The fireflies don't know it, of course, but they also put some sparkle into our summer evenings by lighting up!

Bug Noise: What Makes Crickets Chirp?

Listen! It's a summer night. All is still except for one sound: the rhythmic chirping of crickets. How do these insects sing?

Actually, they are not truly singing at all, since they do not make the noise with their throats. They make it with their wings. There is a special place on a cricket's wings that has tiny ridges, something like the teeth on a metal file. When the cricket rubs its wings together, the ridges on one wing rub against a rough spot on the other, making a chirping sound. At the same time, the wing vibrates and makes the sound louder.

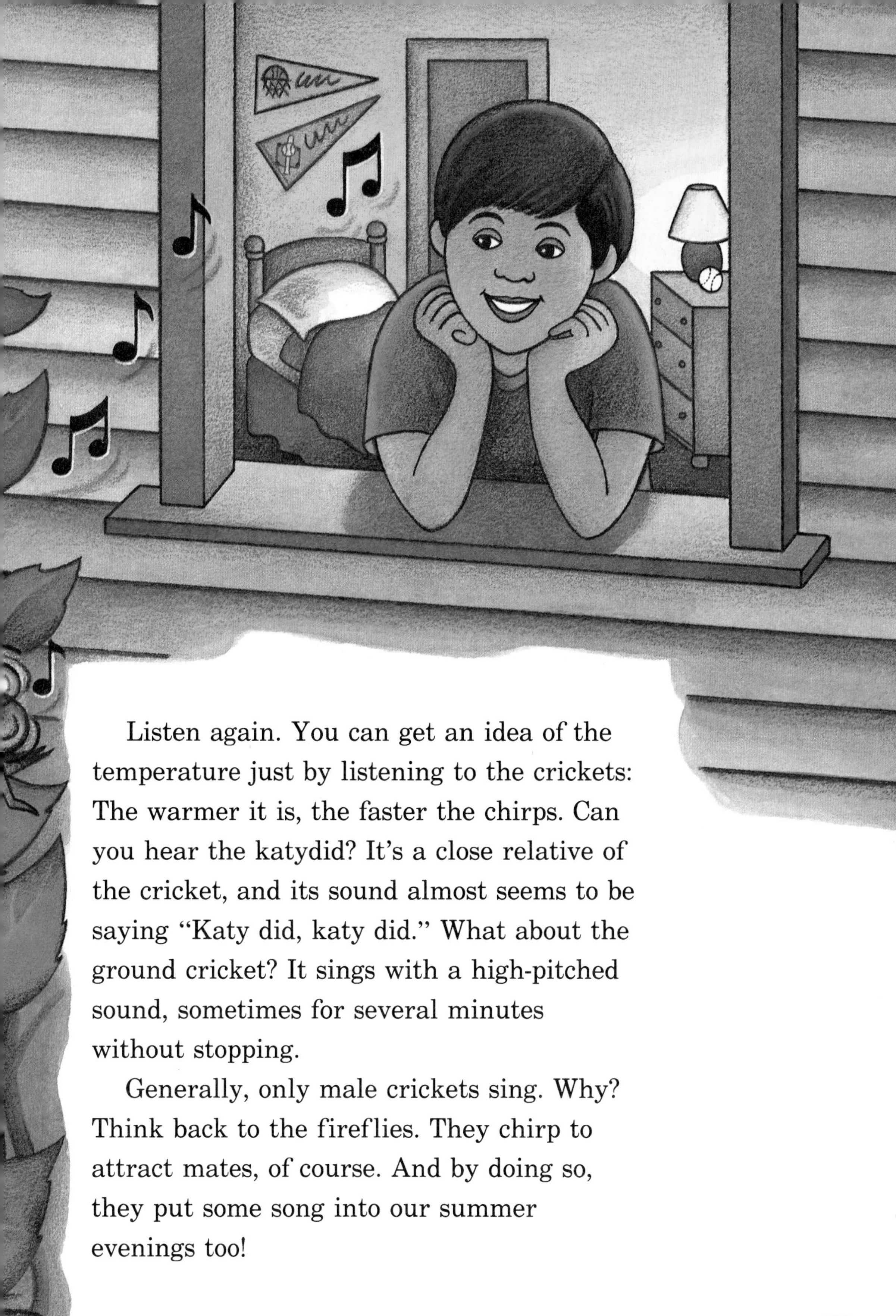

Listen again. You can get an idea of the temperature just by listening to the crickets: The warmer it is, the faster the chirps. Can you hear the katydid? It's a close relative of the cricket, and its sound almost seems to be saying "Katy did, katy did." What about the ground cricket? It sings with a high-pitched sound, sometimes for several minutes without stopping.

Generally, only male crickets sing. Why? Think back to the fireflies. They chirp to attract mates, of course. And by doing so, they put some song into our summer evenings too!

Why Don't Spiders Get Stuck in Their Webs?

An unlucky fly has wandered into a spider's web. The fly is caught in the fine, sticky strands of silk. The more it struggles, the more tangled it becomes. Now the spider is approaching: That fly will be the spider's dinner. Why doesn't the spider get stuck in its own web?

If you look carefully at the most familiar kind of spider's web, which is the orb web made by the garden spider, you'll see that it is shaped like a wheel. Some of the threads go from the center out to the edges, like the spokes on the wheel of a bicycle. Other threads go around in a spiral shape.

The spider has special body parts called spinnerets. These produce thin strands of silk. Some kinds of silk are coated with droplets of a sticky substance like glue, which holds the spider's prey to the web.

When the orb-weaving spider makes a web, it uses plain silk for the spokes. The spider can walk on these spokes without getting stuck.

To make the spiral, the spider uses sticky thread. Web-spinning spiders have three claws on each foot. With these they can

What's this? An occasional bud drops into a spider's web. Many orb-weaving spiders spin a new web every night. Spinning each one takes about an hour.

grasp the dry spokes, avoiding the sticky spiral threads. In addition, the spider covers its legs with an oily substance that keeps them from sticking.

Of course, scientists may discover other reasons why spiders do not get caught in their own webs, too. Meanwhile, these amazing, busy creatures go about their business spinning one of nature's most unusual traps in order to find food.

I Wonder What This Is.

Clue: A pretty necklace or lovely jewel?
Find the answer on page 244.

How does a spider spin an orb web?

Things you need:
dark-colored construction paper
white glue in squeezable bottle
small twigs or leafy branches

1. Glue the twigs or leafy branches on the paper, as if in a frame, and let them dry.

2. Start the outside of your web. Squeeze the glue in a line from one twig to another, and repeat until you have 5 lines, touching the twigs at 5 points. Squeeze the glue slowly so that you get a thin, even line.

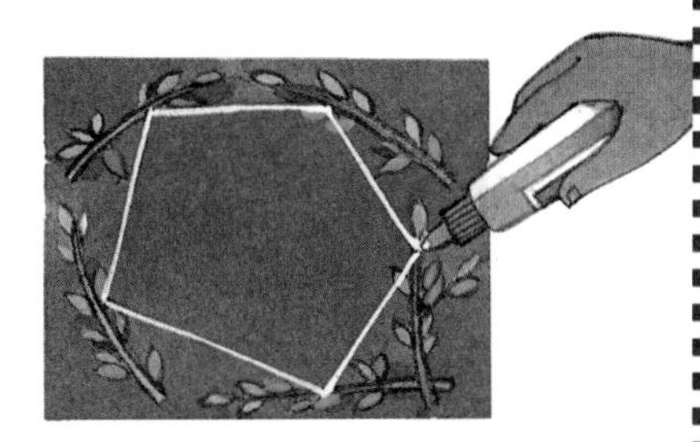

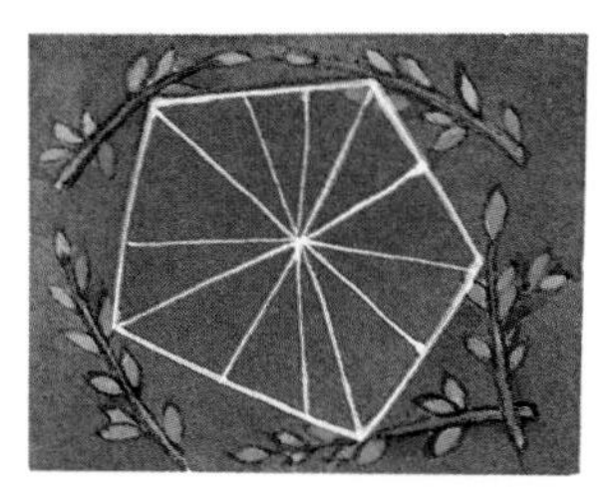

3. Now make the spokes of the web, moving the lines of glue in from the edge and then out from the center. Make 12-16 spokes.

4. Finish your last spoke with the glue at the center. From there, "spin" the lines of glue in a spiral, starting at the center and then moving outward.

5. Next, move to the outer edge of the web and start "spiraling in" again. At this time, a real spider would be spinning the sticky threads that would catch insects. "Spin" over your first spirals after they have dried.

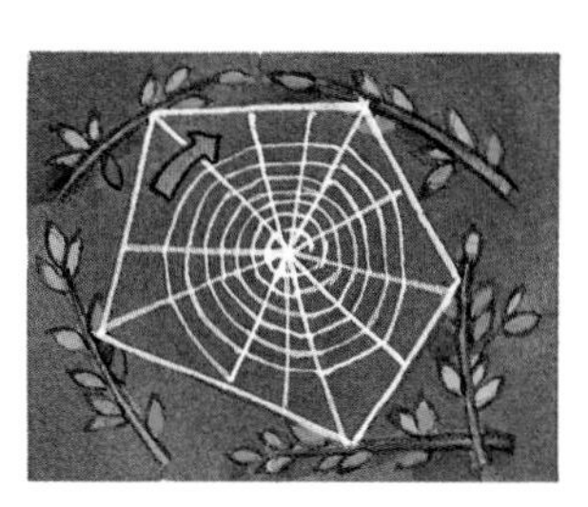

*Get permission first.

Where Are the Baby Squirrels and Pigeons?

It's a lovely spring afternoon. Moms and dads are out walking with their children. Animal mothers and babies are out. There's a duck with her ducklings on the banks of a pond. Up in a tree, a sparrow is feeding her young. But where are the baby squirrels? You don't see very young baby squirrels racing about. And what about pigeons? Are they born full-grown, waddling about? The story of both these creatures has to do with how and where the young are raised.

In the springtime, a female tree squirrel will give birth to a litter of from two to six babies. To get ready, she finds a tree with a hollow in it. She lines it with soft materials like feathers, moss, and pieces of bark. If she cannot find a tree hollow, she may find a bird's nest no longer being used. Or, she may use twigs and branches to build a nest from scratch.

When the squirrels are born they are only about 4 1/2 inches (11.25 centimeters) long and have no fur on their bodies. Their eyes and ears are closed.

By the time the babies are about five weeks old their eyes and ears are open and they have grown a thick coat of fur. A few weeks later they are ready to go out of the nest and explore the world. They learn to climb trees, to run, to find their own food. And then you might see them—playing among the branches, or poking their heads out of a tree hollow. When they are three months old, the young squirrels are out on their own. At about one year of age, they will be ready to find mates and have their own squirrel families.

As for pigeons, they make their nests in out-of-the-way places where you aren't likely to see them. After the female pigeon lays the eggs, she and the male pigeon take turns sitting on them to keep them warm. About 17 days later, the chicks, called squabs, are

born. They look like little balls of yellow fuzz. Their parents feed them a thick white liquid, called pigeon's milk, that comes from a special sac in the pigeon's throat.

Pigeons are the only birds that feed milk to their young. The chick feeds by sticking its bill—and sometimes almost its whole head—into the parent's mouth. After about five days, the parents give less milk. Then they start feeding the squabs food which they, the parents, have spit back out of their own stomachs—unusual but nutritious!

When the squabs are two or three weeks old, they may be as big as their parents. Now they are ready to leave the nest. Soon they will be strong enough to fly—and ready to wobble about with the grown-ups.

How Can Animals Hibernate So Long?

Winter has come to the woods. The ground is covered with snow. It's so quiet! Where are the woodchucks who live here? Where are the other animals? Many are under the ground. They are fast asleep, and they will not wake up until spring. Why do animals sleep through the winter? How can they sleep for such a long time?

For animals, winter can be a difficult time. The cold weather means that there are fewer plants to eat. And the cold makes it difficult to live out in the open. Some animals escape by heading to a warmer place. But many animals stay behind. Some of them survive by going underground and spending the winter in a deep sleep called hibernation (hy buhr NAY shuhn).

Let's watch a female woodchuck. Long before winter arrives, the woodchuck is getting ready. Early in the fall, she digs a winter burrow in which to hibernate. The burrow is like a long hall leading to different rooms: a "bedroom," and a "bathroom." She lines her bedroom with grass and leaves. When the cold weather arrives, the woodchuck goes to her bedroom. She curls up into a ball and falls into a deep sleep.

The woodchuck's body changes in many ways to help her sleep through the winter. Imagine trying to heat your house for the entire winter on only one tank of oil. You couldn't do it unless you turned the temperature control, or thermostat, down to a very low setting. That's what the woodchuck does. Her heart beats only four or five times a minute, compared to about eighty when she is awake. She breathes much more slowly than normal. And her body temperature drops to about half of

what it usually is. By doing these things, the woodchuck's body saves energy.

During the winter the woodchuck will wake up several times to use her small underground bathroom. Then, when spring comes, she will be ready to end her long sleep and leave the burrow again. Although she will be much thinner than when she began hibernating, she will quickly get her strength back by eating new spring plants.

Woodchucks are also known as ground hogs. According to legend, they take a peek outside on February 2 to check for spring!

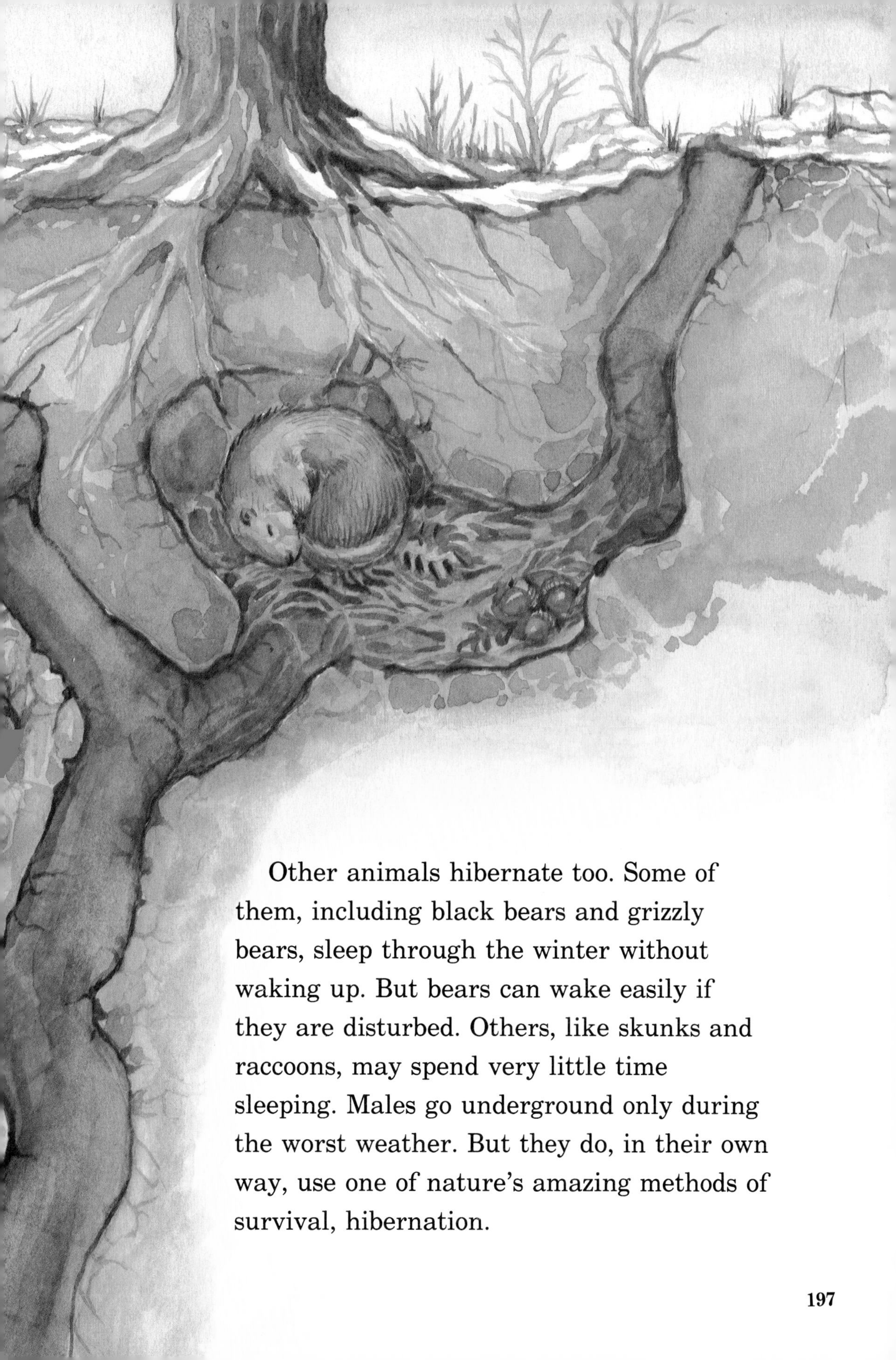

Other animals hibernate too. Some of them, including black bears and grizzly bears, sleep through the winter without waking up. But bears can wake easily if they are disturbed. Others, like skunks and raccoons, may spend very little time sleeping. Males go underground only during the worst weather. But they do, in their own way, use one of nature's amazing methods of survival, hibernation.

Why the Bear Sleeps All Winter

A folk tale from northern Europe

This tale takes place long, long ago, back in the days when people believed in many gods. It so happened that the great god called Ukko came down to earth one day and wandered through the land. Now the gods are very powerful and they live somewhere above, not seen. But this day Ukko dressed as a person, just to see what would happen to him on earth.

Ukko traveled along happily until he came to a river. He wanted to cross it, but there was no bridge. Then he caught sight of a horse grazing in the grass.

"Horse, my friend," called Ukko, "can you please help me over the river?"

"Can't you see I'm busy?" replied the horse with his mouth full of grass. Without another word, the horse trotted away.

Next, to Ukko's delight, a reindeer came bounding past. He called out, "Reindeer, my

friend, won't you please spare a few moments of your time to help me over the river?"

But the proud reindeer answered, "I can't believe you think I would stop, even for a

second. I must leap and run from morning till night. Ask somebody else, you silly man!" Then the reindeer leaped out of sight.

"Alas, I have no choice," thought Ukko sadly. He put his foot into the water to try to cross the river alone. But just then, who should he spot but a great old brown bear plodding along to the river's edge. The bear looked at Ukko with his foot in the river and bellowed, "Good sir, I can carry you over the river. That is, if you are not afraid."

Ukko, relieved, climbed up on the bear's back. The bear swam with him safely to the other side of the river. Once there, Ukko climbed down and thanked the bear for his help, adding, "For your generosity, I shall reward you handsomely!"

"In what way?" asked the bear, surprised.

"While the bitter, cold winds of winter here in the north blow, you my friend, may sleep warm and sound. You need not awaken 'til the gentle breeze of spring passes by your den."

The old bear smiled and told Ukko that he would enjoy the long rest. And this is why the bear sleeps deep through the winter and we do not see him until the sun begins to warm the frozen wood.

How Can Fish Breathe?

Have you ever watched a fish in a pond, darting from rock to rock, swimming here and there? That fish can keep swimming all day. It never has to come up for air. When you stop to think about it, fish can do something that's pretty amazing to us human beings: They can breathe underwater. How do they do it?

People and fish need the same thing: oxygen. But they get it from different places. People get oxygen from the air, using their lungs. When you breathe in, the air goes deep into your lungs, where it meets thin, tiny tubes carrying blood, called capillaries (KAP uh lehr eez). Oxygen in the lungs passes through the capillary walls and enters the blood that's flowing along inside it. The blood flows through your whole body through larger tubes, and oxygen is carried, too. Meanwhile, some of the oxygen you breathe changes into a gas called carbon dioxide (KAHR buhn dye AHX eyed). You get rid of extra carbon dioxide when you breathe out. Blood vessels, all the tubes that carry blood inside you, work together with your lungs as you breathe in and out.

How is a shark different from other fish? Sharks have slits, with no gill covers, for water to flow out after breathing.

A fish, on the other hand, gets its oxygen from the water. Instead of lungs, the fish has special parts called gills. There are two sets of gills, one on each side of the head, usually protected by a bony covering. In order to breathe, the fish opens its mouth and lets some water in. The water passes

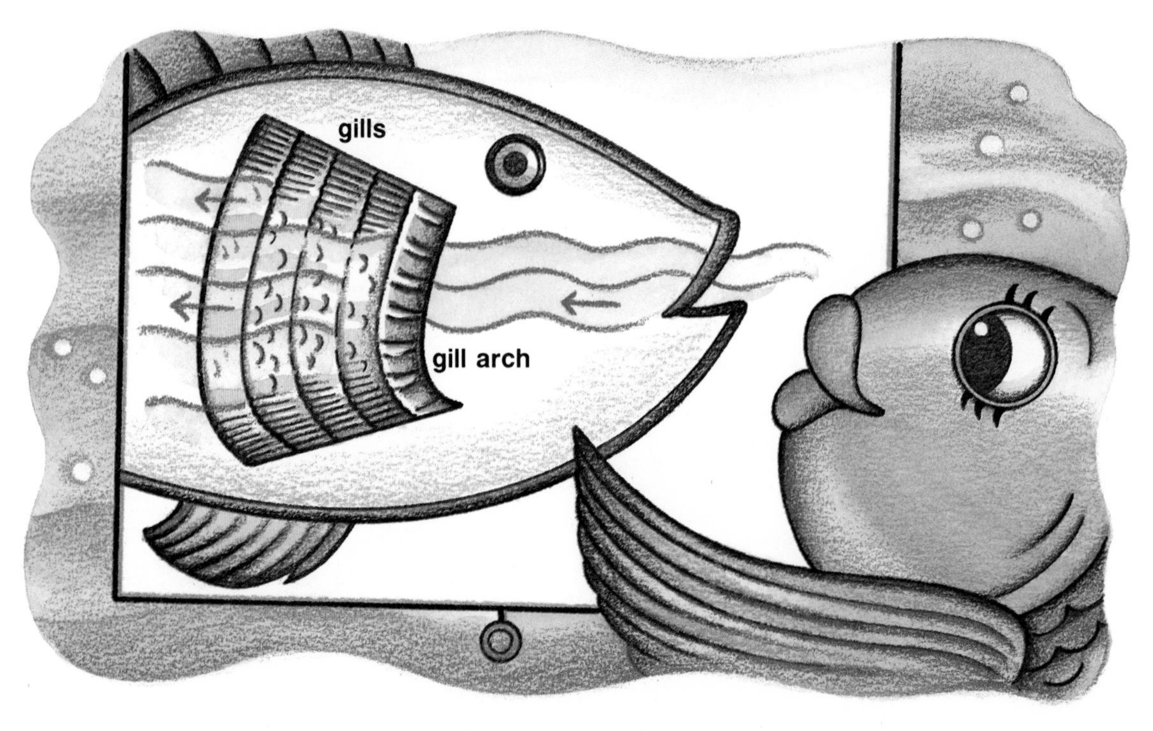

Under the gill coverings of most fish, you would see four fleshy ridges—the gills.

through a valve in the mouth and then flows through the gill sections. When water flows over the gills, oxygen from the water goes into the fish's blood. At the same time, extra carbon dioxide in the blood goes into the water.

There are a few kinds of fish that can also breathe air. One kind is called the lungfish. It has a simple type of lung, in addition to its gills. But most fish would "drown" if you took them out of water. They can't breathe air any better than we can breathe water.

How do whales breathe?

Here is a riddle: What is the name of a big animal that lives in the ocean, looks like a fish, but isn't a fish at all? The answer: a whale. People often think of whales as fish, but really they are mammals. And like all mammals, whales have lungs for breathing air, even though they live in the water. A whale breathes through a hole in the top of its head called the blowhole. In order to breathe, it must swim to the surface so its blowhole is above the water. If the whale dives under again, it must hold its breath—but whales are very good at that. The giant sperm whales can stay underwater for over an hour before coming up for air.

Time out. Unlike most other fish, parrot fish actually stop to rest.

Do Fish Ever Sleep?

Have you ever tried to imagine what it would be like to be a fish? You would think that swimming around all day would make a fish very tired. When people are very tired, they close their eyes and go to sleep. Do fish sleep? Not the way people do, but they rest in a way we could call sleep.

For one thing, most fish don't have eyelids, so they can't close their eyes. After most people fall asleep, they are not aware of the world around them. But fish simply go into a kind of trance and ignore the world.

One kind of fish, called the parrot fish, lives among coral reefs. It finds a safe spot among the coral to spend the night. Then it covers itself with a layer of mucus to shut out the world and not be disturbed. When they rest, some fish are so unaware of the world around them that a careful diver may even be able to touch them. Others are ready to wake up and get out of the way in a hurry at the slightest motion.

Some fish that live out in the ocean are always swimming. Scientists believe they sleep while they are swimming! They flap their tail to move ahead, and then, for just an instant, they "doze off." Then they wake up and move forward again. It doesn't sound like a very good way to sleep, but for these fish it seems to work.

Green Wonders